WILL OUR CHURCH DIS- APPEAR?

MARION
BEST
& FRIENDS

STRATEGIES FOR THE RENEWAL OF
THE UNITED CHURCH OF CANADA

Wood Lake Books

Project Coordinator: Ralph Milton
Project Assistant: Joanne Greenhough
Editors: Jim Taylor, Mike Schwartzentruber
Layout and design: Jim Taylor
Cover design: Lois Huey Heck

Note: All royalties from the sale of this book are being donated to the Mission and Service Fund of the United Church of Canada.

Canadian Cataloguing in Publication Data

Best, Marion., 1932–
    Will our church disappear?

    Includes bibliographical references.
    ISBN 1-55145-049-5

    1. United Church of Canada. I. Title.
    BX9881.B47   287.9'2   C94-910701-8

Published by
Wood Lake Books Inc.
PO Box 700, Winfield, BC
Canada V0H 2C0

Printed in Canada by
Hignell Printing Ltd.
Winnipeg, MB, R3G 2B4

Permissions

Birthing the church

A new church is being born. *It may not be the church we expect or want.* The church of the future may not include our favorite liturgy or hymn, our central theological principle, or even our denomination! God's promises always arrive with surprises in them.

Loren B. Mead
The Once and Future Church
The Alban Institute, 1991, p. 87

Contents

CHAPTER ONE
Gathering for the future

"Today is the first day of the rest of my life."

What a wonderful and terrifying promise! It reminds me of the Chinese character for "crisis" which contains the symbols for both "problem" and "opportunity."

As we approach the 21st century, we are all aware of a number of crises Canada faces. Some say the United Church of Canada is in crisis. Things are changing and they are changing fast. The United Church of Canada, including the congregation I belong to, is faced with both problems and opportunities. I think we can make some creative and faithful choices in these troubling and exciting times. That's the reason for this resource.

I really believe the United Church of Canada has a future. I believe the little congregation I belong to in Naramata village has a future. But if we don't do something creative with the problems, that future could evaporate. I think we have the potential to become the kind of church God is calling us to be.

But how do we make those faithful decisions toward our future? Wood Lake Books offered me a challenge recently. "Select some folks," they said. "People you feel have their pulse on what the United Church is—people who might have some insight into its future."

Of course, almost anyone in the whole church would qualify, but I had to choose nine people out of the several hundreds of thousands who are members of my denomination. It was no easy matter, and the nine I chose certainly are not representative of the vast variety of folk who make up the United Church. None of them were "experts." The one thing we all had in common was a deep sense of caring for this crazy, wonderful denomination and the congregations within it.

We were a diverse and very interesting bunch, and we came at the question of the United Church's future from very different perspectives. We talked from a Friday morning through to Sunday noon at Cedar Glen, a United Church conference center near Bolton, Ontario.

All of our conversation was recorded, all of it transcribed, and a small part of that was edited into what follows. Like all

Ten of us gathered in the lounge at Cedar Glen. Just to the right of the flipchart is author Marion Best. Following around from her are Mardi Tindal, Alan Barss, Faye Wakeling, Pamela Brown, Jim Sinclair, Ed Searcy, Roland Kawano, and Marion Pardy, Phyllis Airhart (hidden).

conversations, it wanders a bit from time to time. On reading the text, I find places where I wish we'd talked more about a particular subject, or an interesting element was left out of our discussion. Still, I felt the group had some really important things to say. Important, not because they were "answers," but because they were useful insights.

Our intention was not to provide a comprehensive analysis. We didn't try to predict the future. We did try to have a discussion that would stimulate your discussion. We wanted to be a model of what a discussion group in your own congregation might be like. So this project becomes useful when you ask some of the questions we asked, but ask them about your own congregation. Your observations may be quite different than ours.

What follows is two things. It's a book you can sit down and just read through. And it is a workbook you can use to hone your own insights. Best of all, you could use this as a workbook with a group from your congregation who might wish to struggle together toward their future. (There are some suggestions for how to do that on page 120.)

How to use this book

Bev Milton agreed to develop study materials so this material could be used more effectively by people in congregations. She included two kinds of questions. There are questions for your personal reflection, as you read what our group said and try to relate that to your own experience. These appear in the outside column of each page. Secondly, Bev has included some questions for group discussion, which are at the end of each chapter.

To get the most out of this resource, however, please organize a group from your congregation to consider your own future and to discern what it is that God is calling your community to do and to be. God speaks to us as individuals, but God most often speaks when the community gathers.

In the end, the important insights are the ones you discover as your congregation listens for God's call into the future.

There are no easy answers. But I believe you will gain some insights. You may receive God's gift of Wisdom, especially if you work with a group in your own congregation.

So here's a sample of what we talked about during those three days. We hope for nothing more than that our conversation will stimulate yours.

The question before us all is simple, and yet terribly complex. How can we, as the United Church, catch the vision of God's future?

It's not an optional question. The book of Proverbs warns us, "Where there is no vision, the people perish." (29:18)

Marion Best: I feel the need for a bit of reassurance. This is a very difficult thing we're undertaking here this weekend. So I went to my Bible and I found a few verses from Isaiah, Chapter 43, starting at verse 18.

> Do not remember the former things,
> or consider the things of old.
> I am about to do a new thing;
> now it springs forth,
> do you not perceive it?
> I will make a way in the wilderness
> and rivers in the desert.

Could those words have provided confidence and reassurance during a struggle your congregation went through?

The beginning of chapter 43 helps put these words in context.

> But now thus says the Lord,
> the one who created you, O Jacob,
> who formed you, O Israel:
> Do not fear, for I have redeemed you;
> I have called you by name,
> you are mine.
> When you pass through the waters,
> I will be with you;
> and through the rivers, they shall not overwhelm you;
> when you walk through fire
> you shall not be burned,
> and the flame shall not consume you.
> For I am the Lord your God,
> the Holy One of Israel, your Savior.

In this scripture, we're not asked to forget everything. But there are some things we can't take with us either. We are called to move forward. There will be some precious things we leave behind, and some painful good-byes to say. But remember: God says, "I will be with you."

And the only way I can do that is to pray. So would you pray with me, silently at first, and then with the words from Psalm 51.

> Create in me a clean heart, O God,
> and put a new and right spirit within me.
> Do not cast me away from your presence,
> and do not take your holy spirit from me.
> Restore to me the joy of your salvation,
> and sustain in me a willing spirit.
> Amen.

Our group

First I'd like to introduce you to the friends that shared the weekend with me, and whom I hope you'll come to think of as your friends, too.

When you really have to struggle with something, is it easier when you're among friends or among strangers?

Alan Barss is married to Colleen. They have three children: Sarah, Michael, and Steven. Alan is a lawyer. Since 1992, he has worked for the Province of Saskatchewan in the Executive Council as an assistant to the Minister of Health. He is a member of St. James United Church in Regina and is active in Saskatchewan Conference.

Alan Barss: I guess I just need to help myself. So my involvement is selfish in that way.

I'm trying to discover the Kingdom of God within me. I go to church to be part of a faith community because there are others there who are trying to do the same thing. I see their struggles and I see their hope. I go to church for me, so that I can become a better person.

Can you help others if you don't help yourself? Is that being selfish?

Mardi Tindal is a United Church layperson and member of Lowville United Church in Burlington, Ontario. She is a co-host of Spirit Connection, The United Church's weekly program on Vision TV. Mardi served the church in various national conference positions for 12 years and now works as a free-lance adult educator and broadcaster. She is Co-Director of York Presbytery's Camp Big Canoe, and lives in

Lowville with her partner Doug, mother Margaret, and children Chris and Alex.

Mardi Tindal: I get my passion from new faces—the energy new people bring into the circle. Every summer it's the energy that teenagers bring into my life. It's such a gift!

Would teenagers feel welcome in your church?

The teenagers and the youth don't have wisdom from many years experience in the same way that perhaps the elders do. But they certainly have energy, and they certainly have ideas and they certainly have questions. I keep wondering if there's a way to really bring them in for what they can give, which is some of that energy. And they have their wisdom too.

Jim Sinclair has been an ordained minister of the United Church of Canada since 1967. He has served the church in various capacities locally and nationally. He lives with his wife, Donna, and their daughter Tracy in North Bay, Ontario. They have two older sons, David and Andy. Jim is part of the pastoral team at St. Andrew's United Church.

Jim Sinclair: There are times, as a minister in a local congregation, when I become really exhausted trying to keep up with people. I've been in the ministry for 27 years and I think I'm just now learning that I have to stay out of the way as people get rolling.

What's the difference between "knowing when to get out of the way" and avoiding responsibility?

There are times when I have been with someone, and the insights come; the person has been able to understand that they are part of the story, that their life is informed by our faith. They are able to make some of the connections as to why that is. I find that very exciting, but very challenging because half the time I can't figure out why or how it happened.

How do you capture that? Capture it in a way that you can transfer it or teach it to someone else?

Marion Pardy is minister of Gower Street United Church, St. John's, Newfoundland. Previously she was Newfoundland/ Labrador Conference Minister for Program and Leadership Development and Program Consultant. Prior to that, she was in Ministry with Children, Division of Mission in Canada. Marion holds an M.A. degree from York University, Toronto, and is currently completing requirements for a D. Min. degree at Boston University.

Marion Pardy: I have a renewed appreciation for biblical preaching. I'm impressed by the large number of people in the congregation who are very well educated and into quite *avant garde* stuff, but their level of biblical understanding is, in some cases, quite primitive.

We do have the dozen people who attend a study group. That's exciting and energizing and good things happen there—for a dozen people.

So my big concern is, how can the preaching be faithful and helpful when the community gathers for worship?

Is a dozen people enough to make all the effort and preparation worthwhile? How many would you consider to be too few?

Phyllis Airhart teaches History of Christianity at Emmanuel College and the Toronto School of Theology. She is the author of Serving the Present Age: Revivalism, Progressivism, and the Methodist Tradition in Canada. *She is now working on a book on the United Church of Canada. Phyllis is a member of Royal York Road United Church in Toronto.*

t.

Phyllis Airhart: As I talk to people my age, I discover that one of the things we struggle with is the need for us to take responsibility for the future of the church. We've been so accustomed to having this strong cohort ahead of us. But there's a generational vacuum in leadership.

My husband, Matthew, and I are among the younger people of the congregation and so we feel some sense of responsibility to develop as leaders. Furthermore, a big part of what I do at Emmanuel is about preparing people to be leaders. So I have to come to terms with myself being a leader, which is really hard for me to do. "Who me? You mean I have to do this now?"

Do you have younger leaders emerging in your church?

Pamela Brown is a physician, counselor and teacher, and church volunteer. She has participated in the work of the church at National, Conference, and local levels, mainly in the areas of sexuality, family and justice issues of violence and sexism. She is a member of St. Andrew's United Church in Halifax, Nova Scotia.

Pamela Brown: I see wonderful things happening, but not when we sit in rows and listen to somebody. I feel really sad for the people who haven't had those tremendous experiences of gathering around a table, or walking on a beach, or wrestling with some piece of worship that we want to get just right. Those are the wonderful moments.

But often there's a great chasm between the life that I experience where I work, and what happens when I go to worship. In my church, where 400 or 500 of us gather on a Sunday, sometimes there is something that connects and miraculously it happens—there is a moment of splendor. And I want more of them because I'm greedy.

Why is it so hard to loosen up and gather in small groups?

Faye Wakeling is the Director of Saint Columba House, an inner-city Outreach Mission of the United Church in Montreal. In a community confronted with long-term poverty, she struggles with the people to understand the roots of our socio-economic crisis and to work for social change. She is a United Church minister involved in women's concerns and aboriginal rights. She chairs the Ecumenical Poverty/Economy Task Force in Quebec. Faye is presently writing a book with women of her community on the sources of hope in the work of social transformation.

Faye Wakeling: Passion-energy comes out of connections with people who are looking for ways to transform society—working for more just conditions. If you want to use religious language, I guess we'd call it "**kin**-dom building." There's real energy in that engagement.

I often find that energy in non-church areas. I see it in the union movement. I see it in the women's movement. I went to a conference with 2,000 women to celebrate the mid-point of the Ecumenical Decade of the Churches in Solidarity with Women. We were from all different backgrounds. We came together and shared very different understandings of what it might mean to be church. And yet we found energy and challenge from the knowledge that the work of God is going on, whether we named it that way or whether the church was involved in it. And I find it hard to know how my church at home is going to connect with that.

Where is the passion in your church? Do you have passionate people?

Ed Searcy is a minister at South Arm United Church in Richmond, British Columbia. His life includes experimenting with the place of children in the worshiping community, chairing the Land Claims Campaign of BC Conference, teaching preaching at the Vancouver School of Theology, and leading summer study programs at Naramata Centre. Ed and Wendy live with their four children: Matt, Joel, Adrianne, and Anneke in Crescent Beach.

Ed Searcy: I know what I can get passionate about, but I'm a bit afraid to talk about it because I am almost always misunderstood. There are so many labels out there and none of them work. What happens when you say that you're "radically conservative" or "conservatively radical." Neither term works. You get both sides dumping on you saying, "Oh no, you think that?" Or both sides running to you saying, "Oh yes, you agree with us!"

Every congregation has its liberals and conservatives. What do you consider yourself?

I can get passionate about raising a million dollars for native land claims and chairing the committee on it. But then I get incredibly upset—passionate—when I encounter United Church institutions that seem to have no Christian memory and are shy about calling themselves **Christian**.

So I seem to be both a liberal and a conservative, and neither. I please and infuriate both sides.

Roland M. Kawano has been working in the Division of Mission of the United Church in the areas of Ethnic Ministries and Multiculturalism, and Mission Support. He has published The Global City *with Wood Lake Books. He has been in pastoral ministry in Toronto, Los Angeles, and Utah. .*

Roland is presently working on a manuscript which explores the roles of the church among the interned Japanese during World War II.

Roland Kawano: My passion focuses on spirituality. As I travel, I find quite different individuals who are into kingdom building, who are very inclusive in all the rest of their lives, who yearn for this thing called spirituality.

Some of them talk about actual healing—spiritual healing. Some of them tell me of their intense prayer. Others talk of their pastoral work in hospitals, where somehow God gives them the grace that people are healed. It's an experiential thing.

Would you feel comfortable with spiritual healing?

You can find spirituality all over the place and it doesn't really matter what the United Church is going to do, it's already inside the people and they've got to follow.

Marion Best is a member of Naramata Community Church in Naramata, British Columbia, where she lives and works as a free-lance educator with church and community groups. She is a past president of BC Conference of the United Church and is currently a member of the Central Committee of the World Council of Churches.

Marion Best: I've just spent five weeks in Africa. This is my second time there. Every time I come back from that other context I see everything through those lenses.

I'm so struck by the global inequities and I wonder, how does my faith relate to that? I don't want to be into charity and I know that the donor-recipient thing has kept people dependent.

Do you have any sense of connection with Christians in other countries?

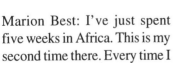

I suppose it's mission that I'm really wanting to talk about. What does it mean to be in mission in a way that's different from the old models of mission? Some of the inequities are just so stark and they hit me so deeply. Those same inequities—maybe not quite as stark—are in my own community here in Canada.

For group discussion:
Which of these people do you identify with the most? How is your experience similar? How is it different?

CHAPTER 2

Our stories

Those of us who gathered at Cedar Glen are all part of the United Church for one reason or another. I assume that those of you reading this book are also part of this denomination in one way or another.

I find it is often really helpful to have groups do some storytelling. And since this is a book about the United Church and its future, it feels important that we should tell our stories of how we got here. This chapter shares the stories we told at our gathering in Cedar Glen. You may hear echoes of your own story in some of them, and I hope that will lead you to do a similar kind of storytelling.

Storytelling is far more than spinning a yarn. As we listen to ourselves tell our own stories and as we listen to others tell their stories, little lights go on: "Ah, so that's why this is so important to me!" Or, "That's why she feels that way!"

I hope you enjoy your storytelling as much as we enjoyed ours.

My ethnic community

Mardi Tindal: As I thought about how I came into the United Church, I found myself thinking of my identity as a granddaughter, a daughter, a mother, a camp director, a teacher and mentor.

I was born into the United Church and with a strong clear sense of the Methodist path that my forebears had taken to get there.

I spent much of my childhood in the home of my maternal grandparents, partly because our house and theirs shared the same farm and gardens, and also because they cared for me when my mother was ill and hospitalized for part of my childhood.

Sundays were very special days. Clean clothes, polished shoes, respectful worship. Decks of cards carefully put away on the shelf.

What are your memories of Sunday and church?

I remember after service and after lunch every Sunday my grandparents would spread out all the offering envelopes on the dining room table. It was their job to do the accounting.

There would never be any alcohol in this house, grace would

always be said at the table, and living a faithful life was really central to them. The centrality of faithfulness was always there when we talked politics too. I learned very early on about their strong political affiliations and commitments. And so I breathed it in.

I was near death a couple of times with asthma attacks. Once (and I guess in some sense I knew this), I'm told, the doctors had given up on me. My mother will say they have no doubt that it was prayer that brought me back. And I have less doubt of that today than I once had.

Have you had an experience similar to that?

It was also very clearly denominational. I remember sitting on the back steps with my grandmother shelling peas and learning about how we were different from that Catholic fam-

What is different for you about the United Church?

ily down the street. This, in a sense, was my ethnic group. In a way it still is. This is my ethnic community even though it's defined differently from other ethnic communities. My grandparents left no doubt in my mind what I was.

It was being part of a Mennonite camp that impressed me the most. But even after a nourishing summer with lots of biblical study and spirited conversation and good singing and good clean living with those Mennonite friends, it wasn't authentic for me. I often think about how they would choose movies or plays to go to. They didn't have the absolutes, no alcohol, no this, no that— at least not in this community. Instead they asked themselves, "Would this be good for my soul?"—discerning questions that I found helpful.

But there was an underlying bias. God wasn't in the world as much as God was in their community. So they had to keep watch and protect themselves from contamination. And in some way that was inconsistent with what I had learned in my United Church upbringing. They were a little more exploratory about sin and evil, but it wasn't my path.

And I decided then that this was my path that God had given

me to take care of. And I really believe that God would be sad-dened, if not diminished, if the United Church of Canada per-ished.

Has God called you to a particular path?

You belong in this church

Phyllis Airhart: I wasn't born into the United Church. I studied my way into the United Church.

My mother came from a Baptist family which never attended the Baptist church. She was very Baptist in her world view. My father smoked and this was always a sore point.

Do you have other de-nominations in your background?

Most often, I went to church with the relatives of my father's family whose kids were involved in an evangelical church. I think I've absorbed that rural Maritime evangelical piety. I still appreciate that, even though I've moved beyond it. But I still value a lot of what that gave me.

In university I found that I didn't fit anymore. I studied my way into the United Church with a professor who taught me con-temporary theology. When I talked to him about what I thought about certain things, he would say, "Phyllis, **you** belong in the United Church." That's where my "warm piety and a social compassion" belonged. As I developed professionally, I came to realize he was probably right, even though the Anglican liturgy really drew me. There's part of me that loves the beauty of the Anglican liturgy.

I was drawn to the church that I learned about as I worked on my dissertation on Methodism. I felt drawn to the United Church at its best. I find a mix of the prophetic and the priestly aspects of liturgy, combined with the possibilities of cultivating personal pi-ety. That's important to me as well—that balance of social jus-tice, personal piety and real possibilities of cultivating the wor-ship life of a congregation.

Do you like your congre-gation? Why?

I really like my congregation—Royal York Road in Etobicoke. It's a caring community that has a strong sense of outreach to the local community and also to the wider world—through the Mission & Service fund.

I am drawn to a church that asks hard questions even if I don't always like the answers that the church comes up with. I value the willingness to struggle with those hard issues.

Is God really calling?

Ed Searcy: How did I come into the United Church? I was born. It's as simple as that.

What were you born into?

I was born in 1954 at Naramata Centre, a United Church training facility in the Okanagan Valley of British Columbia. My uncle, Bob McLaren, was the founder.

We were not a church family to start with. But my uncle was. So my dad met my mom at a United Church camp at Cultus Lake. Apparently they met because both of them snuck behind the same tree for a smoke.

So I was born into the United Church, although my parents, I think, were loved into it. Theirs was the discovery of a gracious family in the church and they've spent their lives in the United Church ministry. I grew up going to Naramata Centre. I was the oldest son and lived out all the oldest child stuff.

For me the big struggle was the question, "Is this really what God is calling me to do, or I am just living out a role?" The answer is probably both.

What are your first memories of church?

My first memory of the church is sitting in a tiny church in Lillooet, which is on the Fraser River in B.C., and throwing up. I remember that, but I don't know why. And I can remember being allowed to ring the church bell.

My dad was the minister. He would come down the aisle on the way into church and we would sit by the aisle. Dad would put his hand on my shoulder as he went by.

I saw all the good stuff about the church, but I began to realize the dark side too. I found myself growing away from it—finding some distance.

I had grown up hearing my parents and my aunt and uncle say the church was such a wonderful place. Then how did I live with all that stuff that wasn't so wonderful about the church?

I find it difficult to deal with that dark side, at times, with peers in the ministry, older people, or other folks who just seem to be in love with the church. I always search out folks who can laugh at it, cry about it, and have some distance from the church.

So I've come to terms with the church, I think. At least more than I had ten years ago.

What is not good about your church?

A far from perfect church

Marion Pardy: I've been a member of the United Church almost since I was born. I was born on May 9 and was baptized almost immediately. That is very significant for me. I feel like the United Church is my home. I have been involved in the church ever since, so I have 50 plus years in the United Church.

Were you baptized? When?

I remember really enjoying Sunday school as a child. Back when I was four or five years old, I had to travel by train to go to the hospital for surgery. I remember waking up on Sunday morning and crying because I wanted to go to Sunday school. Part of that may have been wanting to go home as well.

I had a very conservative church upbringing but there was a sense that the church was about something much larger than this building or this community where we lived. I learned that mostly through Mission Band—learning the stories about the poor people in other countries who didn't have schools and didn't have hospitals. My sense of what mission is about is quite different now, but the Mission Band instilled in me a sense that the church was about concern for the world.

I also remember my grandmother putting her 25 cents in one side of the envelope saying, "This is for us," and 25 cents in the other saying, "This is for others." And I tend to do the same.

I was really very conservative. I remember a staff member

How much do you give to the church each week?

at the Atlantic Christian Training Centre showing us some dance steps for some of the Christmas carols. I was shocked. I thought, "If that's what you have to do to be in the United Church, I'm getting out of it."

I attended Covenant College (and I'm skipping over a few years) where I had a real crisis of faith. One day in class I threw my pen across the room and left a Systematic Theology class saying, "I can't cope with this, I'm getting out." The professor was teaching all of the different theories of the atonement and the resurrection. We had an assignment to write on that theme. I concluded that I did not, could not, write with any integrity on any of those topics. So the best thing for me was to leave the school and the church.

Have you been tempted to leave your church because of your beliefs?

Doug Shanks, in his wisdom, suggested to me then that if I could not write on any of those topics, maybe I could write on the "God is dead" theology.

"Oh yeah, I can write on that, no problem," I replied. So I wrote on "God is dead" and concluded, after great personal struggle, that there were as many valid reasons for accepting the idea of God as there were for rejecting it.

In the '70s I went through another crisis. This time it was not a faith crisis; it was an institutional crisis. In my mind the conservatives had a monopoly on the church. I thought, "I really don't want to be part of this." So I identified about half a dozen people who I thought were okay and still working for the institution. I asked them, "What's a wonderful person like you doing in this church?" So I sorted through that one too, and came out of my struggle with a sense that even though it was far from perfect, I could still identify with the United Church.

Why do you stay in the church?

A warm church

Did your parents go to church?

Pamela Brown: I grew up as an Anglican in a small town in the south of England. My family belonged to a tiny, ancient, little church that always had a sort of musty cold feeling to it. I spent a lot of time there, to please my dad mainly. He was a dear gentle person who was deeply devoted to the church. In a very quiet, unobtrusive way, he'd be there stoking the boilers so at least the major chill was off the place on Sunday morning in the winter. He and my mother were convinced that going to church was the right thing to do, so I did it.

I don't remember any sense of being spiritually connected but it was a good place to be. The flowers were lovely and it just felt right. But that was really all it was.

When I went to university in London, to study medicine, my "significant other" at the time took me to hear John Stott at All Souls, Langham Place.

So I went and listened to John Stott and was swept along in a wave of...well...for one thing the church was warm. It felt sort of prosperous. For about six months it seemed like an important place to be. But I kept waiting for something to happen that reached inside of me and it never did.

Have you ever had a religious experience? Do you want one?

I married Douglas, a Canadian, and we came to live in Halifax. We lived right across the street from his home church. But eventually we became involved with St. Andrew's United down the street—especially when our family came along. It seemed as if St. Andrew's would be a good spot for our daughters to begin going to Sunday school. By now I was a full-time homemaker (I'd given up my medical practice) and did a fair bit of volunteer work. We went to church but we weren't involved with the church. Doug was on the Board of Stewards and I went to the coffee parties.

In the meantime—this was in the early '70s—I became very much involved with the Family Planning Movement and did some teaching around sexuality in schools and medical schools. Lo and behold, in the late '70s my church, the United Church, started talking about sexuality too. Finally my Monday to Saturday life and my Sunday life came together.

In 1980 I was asked to help work on the national church's sexuality reports. I began to feel that the United Church was not only comfortable, it was exciting, it was dynamic, it was challenging, and it was home.

Then I was asked to be a member of the national committee that did the sexual orientation study. It was actually only three years between the time we first got together in '85 and the time we met finally at Victoria in '88 during the General Council meeting.

Are you bothered by these issues? Why?

When that sexuality and sexual-orientation work was being done I had some very, very rough moments indeed. The leadership in my local congregation was on the other side of the issue and galloped out of the United Church in fine fashion very shortly after the Victoria General Council. That was a difficult time.

Were you tempted to leave in 1988? At any other time? Over what issue?

Some of the situations were the most prickly places that I have ever been in my life. I thought things were going to be thrown at me, such was the hostility that I encountered. But I was personally convinced that it was crucially important work and I still have this enormous sense of privilege of having been part of it and part of what followed.

In the meantime I went back to being a doctor. My medical work is still very much around sexuality and teaching. Around 1990 I was invited to take some part-time responsibility at the Atlantic School of Theology. That has been a nurturing community for me too.

Does your church push you to ask hard questions?

I've been lucky enough for my faith life and my work and my family life and volunteer life and friendships all to sort of mix together. I think that's been the gift for me of the United Church, which has not only allowed this, but has affirmed it and given me opportunities which are just beyond price.

Wanting to make a difference
Alan Barss: I'm struck by the fact that I have no clue what my family's roots are beyond the United Church. Not a clue. As far as I know they're all United Church. I have no recollections at all about any sort of Methodist or Presbyterian heritage.

Did your family discuss religious roots?

It didn't matter. It wasn't a topic of conversation in my family. We were just United Church and that was it.

I was born into the United Church. My father is a United Church minister, although he wasn't at the time that I was born. He worked for SaskTel right out of high school, but in 1967 he decided that he really needed to do something different with his life. He wanted to work with people,

What do you want for your life?

he wanted to help, he wanted to make a difference.

At least I think that's what it was. We've never really talked about it, you know. It was just right for him to do and he moved us all to Saskatoon and went to university.

Like my father, I went to work for SaskTel right out of high school. It took him 13 years to realize that he needed to do something else. It only took me 11. But I decided that I really needed to do something more with my life than fixing telephone equipment and computers.

I wanted to work with people. Unlike my father I made a deliberate choice **not** to go into ministry. Living in a manse in rural Saskatchewan I knew there was a lot of baggage that goes with rural ministry, and I really didn't want to pick up that baggage.

I didn't think becoming a minister could accomplish what I wanted to do. That may have been possible in 1968 for my father, but I didn't think that was still true in 1988. I sensed that maybe church was becoming less and less important in society and that society was becoming more and more secularized.

If I wanted to make a difference—if I wanted to be a factor in society—then I had to be in the secular world and not in the religious world. So I went to law school and became a lawyer and embarked upon a path which ultimately took me into politics. That's where I've been for the last two years.

Do you make a difference? How?

Making connections

Faye Wakeling: I was born into the United Church. I grew up in a small town in southern Ontario where the church was all that was going. It was always very hard to separate the ethos of small town Ontario from the church.

It was a homogeneous town. Nothing but Christians. No people of color. I never met a Jewish person or any person of color until I went off to university.

My mother was very involved in the CGIT. That turned me on to the church, because when I was a little kid she took

Did you know people of other cultures and races when you were a child?

groups of girls off to weekends. They had a wonderful time and I'd get to tag along if I was lucky. I always looked forward to being old enough to get into that kind of thing.

I went to church on Sunday morning. We had Sunday school in the afternoon so you spent your whole day there. There was a tremendous sense of belonging and support. People cared for you. But in spite of that there were two topics you didn't talk about— faith and sex. There was no prayer life. Even though my mother was committed to every church organization and worked her whole life in the church, these were private things we didn't talk about.

The highlight of my experience in church was being in a choir with 125 children every Sunday and having that spine-tingling sense that in a group you can sing better than by yourself. That's my first corporate sense of what "church" means.

What was the highlight of your childhood church experience?

I came into theology late in life, after having been in medicine for a while, then in physiotherapy, and then at home with my children. I was in my mid-30s before I went into theology. That started things changing.

A Catholic woman professor started a pilot project on feminism. That was 1974, I think. We had a three-hour dialogue with Mary Daly that blew my mind. She raised questions I had never dared to look at. I couldn't deal with most of it at the time. But that started a lot of questioning and seemed to give me the right to really push at some of the things that I had simply accepted until then.

Do you question religious ideas or simply accept them?

From that point on my faith journey became more tied to what I learned from third-world countries—from peoples in which I saw incredible struggle but wonderful faith—faith that was rooted in their struggles, rooted in their day-to-day need to be able to find some way through the horrors with which they were confronted.

I had a hard time making connections with what I experienced in our church. As part of my quest, I did a student placement year at Saint Columba House, an inner city mission, where I am now working. There I began to see our society, and what it means to be faithful, from a different perspective. The strength of community, their continual struggle for justice and sharing that has no limits, brought about a different kind of conversion for me.

What churches normally do
Jim Sinclair: In our congregation we measured the church year, not by color or liturgy, but by which supper we were going to

have. And I loved the church suppers.

What was your favorite church-supper dish?

It wasn't just the food. It was the excitement around going down to this particular event at that particular season of the year. We'd meet my dad there after he'd come directly from work.

It was a church where the minister of the day had a great influence on me. One in particular—Earl Lautenschläger. You either loved him or you hated him. I can remember the day that his secretary was telling my father that she heard him in the office saying, "Damn! I guess I'll have to do it myself." At that time, so many kids had been turned back from Queens, from Western, from U. of T., that he felt it was time to start a northern Ontario university.

I can remember being at the first convocation of Huntington University, and Leslie Frost, the Premier of Ontario, saying, "The reason I'm here is because that man Lautenschläger walked past my secretary one day into my offices and said, 'Mr. Premier, we need a university in northern Ontario.'"

Did you have heroes you admired?

So I just thought that's what churches normally did.

I was also raised in the YMCA and so I assumed that I would go to Sir George Williams College and I would become a YMCA secretary and live happily ever after.

But I didn't want to lock myself into something, so when I got to university I began to explore. I knew I couldn't be a minister because I just couldn't see myself like Earl Lautenschläger. So that solved that problem.

Then I discovered I wasn't satisfied in social work; I wasn't satisfied in the YMCA. These institutions didn't seem to get to the things that I wanted to come to grips with in the lives of people, or in my own life. Someone said, "Well, why don't you think in terms of a mission field?" And I went off to Saskatchewan, right in "Dances-With-Wolves" country on the Montana border. That's where I really felt I got yanked into the church by these wonderful, conservative, ranching families.

How did you get "yanked" into church?

And boy did I see! I could recognize out there what I experienced back home. I saw it better because it was in another place—what it was to work cooperatively, what it was to live in very hard times, what it was to start with practically nothing. I remain in touch with these folks even today.

On to ordination. I ended up in northern Quebec in Schefferville and I felt absolutely unequipped. So it was off to the States for a couple of years of further study.

I got down there and we looked around for a church to go to. We were unsatisfied with a lot of the options—Presbyterian, Methodist. The one we were most comfortable with was the Unitarian.

We ended up driving an hour every Sunday to go to a church because the minister there had been condemned by President Nixon. This was during the Vietnam war. We figured something must be right in that congregation.

But finally the time came to come home, and as we headed north on the Pennsylvania Turnpike, Donna and I both started singing the doxology! I couldn't really articulate what I was coming back to but I knew I came back to a very strong sense of what my faith was.

Are you glad to be a Canadian?

Grandma gifted my mother

Roland Kawano: I was born in a church that became the United Church of Christ, USA. Congregationalists, formed by missionaries who came around the horn from Boston, Harvard, and Yale and formed a church in the Hawaiian Islands.

Do you think the churches of other races and cultures are equally valid?

When I was ordained my dad laid his hands on me, and he reminded me that I had been dedicated before the table of the Lord as an infant. There was no infant baptism in that church.

I grew up in a Congregationalist Church. But the real story is why I'm in a church at all. I have to go back a generation. My forebears on my mother's side came from Japan to southern California and worked in a little farm there. No Buddhist temple there, and of course we were all Buddhists.

My maternal grandmother, believing that her last child needed spiritual education, literally gave or gifted my mother to the local Sunday school. I don't understand why grandma did this. I don't think my mother understands why grandma did this. Grandma just did this. Grandma gifted mother to the church. It may have something to do with the compassionate heart of Buddhism.

Could you "give" your child to the church?

When I was going to seventh grade my parents placed me in an Episcopal college prep school. We call them Anglicans. I was an altar boy. That's how I learned.

I had planned, in my undergraduate work in Wheaton College, Chicago, to become a medical missionary. I felt that's what God was calling me to. And I went to medical school.

But the calling began to fall apart as my perceptions about mission activity became stronger and I became very disgruntled about the whole process. I wasn't sure what I was looking for but I wasn't satisfied.

Going to medical school in that era of American history is important because many of my colleagues were in medical school so that they would not go to Vietnam. So when I came to the decision to leave medical school I had to face the consequences, which were that I might be drafted. After much soul-searching, I became a conscientious objector.

How do you feel about war?

I think God asked me to do this work with ethnic ministries here in Canada because of my experience in Hawaii and the model of all these different kinds of people living together. The United Church of Christ is the largest Protestant church in Hawaii, and has the longest history. It is the church that really founded the religious structure of the islands.

I think I realized, coming from this whole Asian Pacific relational ethic, that what I was experiencing in this church system was something extremely Oriental. You cannot do one thing in the United Church without bowing down to somebody else! And it goes on constantly until some form of consensus happens and then we can move.

Much of my work is around congregational development among minorities, ethnic ministries, and all the issues that go with that. I have come to sense that what we have developed in the United Church of Canada is the equivalent of what historians call the "family compact." In Ontario history, the family compact was the "in" group. It was a family network—everybody married into everybody else, through business, through church—that controlled

Is there a clique in your congregation? Are you part of it?

politics, economics, church, everything.

And so my kind of work with minority congregations hits up against a United Church "family compact." The metaphor of the United Church may be "inclusion," but it is inclusion into a family compact, and that's created a lot of issues for ethnic and other peoples.

A mystical experience

What have children taught you?

Marion Best: I wasn't born into the United Church. A child led me into the church.

Although my parents were not involved in a church when I was a child, they wanted my brother and me to go to Sunday school. So we were sent off to the closest Sunday school which was one of the more evangelical, almost fundamentalist, Baptist mission field churches.

I remember feeling very warm about the place. I felt like

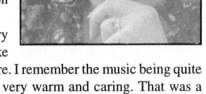

I was loved and cared for there. I remember the music being quite joyful and the people being very warm and caring. That was a really good place for me for quite a few years.

I also remember getting a lot of Bible stories. There was a lot of Bible work and very colorful take-home leaflets. I can still see the pictures on those story leaflets.

But when I got to be about twelve I started asking questions, and I can remember saying once to a teacher, "Can you really believe that? Do you really believe that?" I was told, "Don't ask those questions. Just take everything on faith."

Why do the young people you know leave the church?

I think I stayed about a year after that and then decided I just didn't need this. And, because there wasn't really any family reinforcement, I just left. It was as if they said, "Yeah, you've probably gone long enough. Okay, you don't need to go anymore."

I didn't go near church again until I was a nurse. And there I came across some life-and-death issues. I remember holding a three-month-old baby who died. And I felt, "There's got to be somebody who can help me deal with this kind of thing."

Some friends of mine went to a United Church so I thought, "I'll go with them." My first thought was that the music was kind of dull after my experience with the evangelicals. But in nursing you don't get many Sundays off and so I never really did make a life in that congregation.

When Jack and I were married his family was involved in the United Church and so when we asked, "Where will we be married?" we decided, "The United Church, I guess." Friends of mine had gone to the United Church so I thought it must be all right.

Not that Jack was really involved, but his family was, particularly his mother whom I just adored. A wonderful woman. I felt that somehow she embodied a lot of what the faith was about. So we were married in the United Church and I think went half a dozen times in the first year that we were married. But we didn't go again on a regular basis.

The birth of our first child was a mystical experience for me. That was almost 40 years ago.

It was before natural childbirth had become more common. I remember being quite rebellious about that: "I'm going to have this baby with no anesthetics because I want to be awake for this." (This also tells you something about my wanting to be in charge of everything.)

So I was awake. In fact, the doctor didn't even get there. One of my classmates delivered the baby.

But as I was having that child, a phrase went through my mind. "I have touched the hem of his garment."

Obviously this came from the stories I had heard in that little Sunday school. Where else would it have come from? It wasn't everyday language.

And I knew I wanted this child to be baptized. I wasn't baptized. But I wanted this child to be baptized and I wanted this child to grow up in a Christian community in a way that I hadn't really experienced. So I trotted off to the minister who had married us and said, "I would like to have the baby baptized."

This was just at a time when the United Church was saying, "We will only baptize the children of members." I didn't know that then. But I will always remember the graciousness of this minister. That sent me a message about acceptance and inclusion, and about a willingness to hear my story. And about not going by all the rules. Instead he said, "This is what you promise in a bap-

Have you had a mystical experience? Had you thought of childbirth as a mystical experience?

What does baptism mean to you?

tism. How does that sound to you?"

And so we talked about that. He said, "Well, what about joining the church?"

"No, I'm not ready to do that." And then I realized that saying vows for my baby's baptism would be a commitment to join the church. But he didn't push me about that either.

What do you, as a congre-gation, promise when there is a baptism?

So Cathie was baptized. I realized that I took those vows around raising this child in a Christian environment very seriously. As an adherent first, and then later as a member of the congregation, I took seriously what it meant when I vowed that I would help nurture other children in the Christian faith.

So in many ways, my entry into a deeper understanding of the faith was through a child. I began teaching Sunday school just at the time the New Curriculum arrived on the scene and so was part of a group studying the *Word and the Way*. It felt like an explosion of learning in the United Church. I felt as if I got in on a wave.

The time was right. At least, they felt like important times for me. The whole idea of team teaching was catching on, and I realized I wasn't just teaching children, but children were teaching me. We were learning from each other. I think I was a better parent because of that. Later, I took a job at Naramata Centre, and that became an introduction to ways of working more collegially.

The congregation I belong to is quite diverse. There are a number of us who would probably be described as more "liberal" than the others. But there are also people who are not much different than some of those folks from my childhood Sunday school. Folks who say they don't want to question—just take things on faith. But somehow we manage to be one congregation together.

That's always been my hope—that somehow we could respect our differences. If those people didn't want to question, well, that's where they are. But I need to question, to search, and I need some people I can do that with. We can still be part of one congregation together and we can still come together in worship.

I have this deeply held belief that somehow we can be together with diversity. But that's where it hurts the most at this point. It feels as if, as a church, we're becoming fragmented. We may have too many special interest groups. Somehow the feeling of the whole is slipping away.

That's part of what the United Church has always been.

I've always believed there will be a place there for me. There needs to be a place for each one of us. And so I feel sad because maybe that's not going to be the way it is in future.

How can you be both together and diverse in one congregation?

For group discussion:

With which of these people do you most identify? How is their story the same or different from yours?

Have you, as a congregation, told your story? Who can tell you, as a congregation, the most about your congregational history?

CHAPTER 3

Identity—who are we?

When we told our stories about the United Church and how we got involved, we talked about the things that mattered to us. We learn about our own identity when we tell our own stories, and we learn about others as we listen to theirs. We're talking about our "identity." Who are we, anyway?

After we told our stories at Cedar Glen, we talked some more about how the United Church has been significant to us. For some, it was the significance of the national church, for others it was the life in their home congregation. For me it was both.

Another word we used was "ethos." What is the style, the personality, the intangible something that happens when we are trying to be the church together? We were never completely sure if what we were talking about applied only to the United Church, or only to our own congregation, or to other denominations, or to society in general.

As you'll see from what follows, sometimes our sense of identity was mostly that we all feel fragmented. We're all confused and a bit afraid. Sometimes that can lead to wishful thinking.

Roland Kawano and Faye Wakeling ask each other the basic question: "Who are you, anyway?"

There are no easy or pat answers. But by struggling together and listening carefully to each other, we could see a little more clearly. At least, that's what happened at Cedar Glen. I hope it will happen for you in your group as well.

Jim Sinclair: It's typically United Church that we're even asking these kinds of questions!

Mardi Tindal: There were gentle echoes of the social gospel aspect of the United Church in what we said earlier when we described our church background. I think that social gospel ethos is still there. And I think we're going through a bit of grief that we're not the political voice—we're not the corporate voice—that we used to be. So much of who we were in the United Church of Canada was a political voice. It has been said that if you want to get anything changed in Canada recruit a half dozen United Church women and a few NDP folks!

Is this the United Church you have known?

Faye Wakeling: I think you're right. We don't have that voice now and we're hankering after it and wondering how we will find identity in new ways that still come out of that same commitment to gospel values of justice.

One very concrete example of what it means to see the United Church in action was at the time of the Oka crisis. There was an incredible involvement of all levels of the United Church. We did not see that from any other denomination. I don't mean there were not other people involved. But in terms of a denominational commitment, it was quite extraordinary.

We found that we had the structures and the flexibility and support of the church to act in a

Why us?

My congregation was in pain. Twenty years ago, they told me, they had to put chairs in the aisles to accommodate the overflow. Now a hundred or so people sat scattered around a sanctuary designed to seat 600. "We had 500 children in our Sunday School," they declared. Now we had a total of nine children among all the families in our congregation.

"What have we done wrong?" was the question they dared not say out loud. Some looked at me as though it was the minister's fault. I began to wonder how much of it was.

Our neighbor congregations reported the same story. I had books on my shelf that told me the Protestant mainline denominations were losing members all over North America. Knowing the statistics, however, did not answer the question, "Why us?"

Clair Woodbury
from *100 Ways to Be the Church*
Wood Lake Books, 1991

way that wasn't possible through the other denominations. And we constantly tried to make this an ecumenical involvement. There were many calls to every denomination. But that is also part of the United Church identity—not to want to be there alone. Yet to find that our structure gave us that flexibility and support is really quite unique. For me that's a real highlight of what it meant to be United Church at that time.

Marion Best: The Oka crisis does point out some of the complexities every time we get involved in these ways, doesn't it? When I think of the free-trade debate and the different perspectives on that, it's hard to make the distinction between getting involved in the issues and taking sides. How do you be informed—be a servant community—in a way that doesn't immediately align you with a particular political party or a particular position? The United Church has taken those risks. Now we have to deal with the fall-out.

How is the United Church active in your own community?

Social gospel

Ed Searcy: I took that social gospel perspective for granted when I was a student intern in Knowlton and Waterloo, Quebec, and when I was settled in the prairies. And even now in a big suburban congregation.

There's always been a significant group of people in each place really involved in the social justice movement in the United Church. Then there's a larger group that's not really involved but very open and accepting and ready to talk and listen. Then there's a smaller group that's hostile to the whole idea. Across that whole spectrum, we get reactions whenever the United Church is involved in any issue.

Sometimes it's good to get a bit of perspective. I got some help in the 1980s from a retired minister in my congregation at Crescent United. Frank Runnalls told me about all the pain that he went through in the Kootenays in British Columbia in 1932 after B.C. Conference passed a resolution supporting unemployment insurance—about how difficult it was for him as a young minister to cope with the anger that was generated. How could the United Church possibly do that?

Does the church make you angry sometimes?

It was such a gift to have Frank as a mentor, because in the last four years, I've been hearing the call to resolve the native land-claim questions. And it's good to know that the first missionaries who came to B.C. spoke out and said the land-ownership question needed to be addressed. So 100 years later it still hasn't been dealt with.

That social justice stance is one of the things that people who are not in the United Church take for granted about us. They say, "Oh, there goes the United Church again!" or "We're proud, we're not United Church people." But there are others, who have no connection with the United Church, who really affirm the things we do. Like after the 1988 General Council and the gay ordination issue, we had people telling us they were really glad the United Church had that kind of courage.

We clearly think this is right to be doing this. But we've almost forgotten if this is really biblical. Are we really a church, or is this just a good thing to believe? We may have developed some collective amnesia about what it means to be church.

Do you usually agree with what the United Church says? Would you like it sometimes to stay out of things?

Phyllis Airhart: I'd like to know whether our sense of identity is shifting as congregations begin to feel that they can't hold on to all of those diverse parts. We used to take it for granted that we held together as a United Church. We **celebrated** our differences.

Marion, you were describing that. You talked about the different people in your church, and your vision of them all staying together despite their differences.

I have a general sense that, not only in the church but in our culture generally, we are in a decentralizing mode. That makes it more difficult for the church nationally to speak on behalf of any particular group within the church.

How does your congregation feel when the church speaks out, nationally?

The focus becomes much more on what our local congregations are doing. That's a problem that a lot of denominations are facing now, but maybe we feel it a little more acutely in the United Church because we've tried and succeeded for a significant part of our history to be able to juggle those differing perspectives. Are we going to have to choose? That's very frightening to me because I don't want to make that choice.

Do we all have to think and act the same to be a "united" church?

Powerful voices
Jim Sinclair: I think the choice happens right in the local congregation. I remember that after Clarke MacDonald was elected Moderator by the General Council, he went right into Archambault Prison. He was asked by the Francophone prisoners to be an arbitrator to inspect their situation. Clarke was one of our strong na-

Marion Pardy and Phyllis Airhart consider the theological implications of United Church justice policies

Can you see yourself, and your congregation, assuming the responsibilities that used to be left to national leaders?

tional leaders, like Ray Hord and Jim Mutchmor. We could all sit back and those people in effect "carried the can."

The Women's Missionary Society did a lot of that too. They spoke and acted for us, and we were happy with that.

Now it isn't possible. Decentralization is occurring. That puts these choices and struggles right in front of people in our own congregations, and that can be very threatening and very divisive. How do you raise the confidence of local people to do what our national leaders did at an earlier time?

Marion Best: The national church used to publish a resource book every year from the Board of Evangelism and Social Service. That Board influenced what was preached in a lot of congregations. The book was very topical. They published a new one every year.

I remember Ray Hord speaking out against American involvement in Vietnam, and in favor of the draft dodgers coming into Canada. He died from a heart attack when he was still quite young, and I wonder how much that attack was attributable to the abuse he took, not only from United Church folks but from beyond.

Most of the speaking out on social justice issues has moved over to the ecumenical coalitions now. I think that's quite appropriate—that it be done ecumenically. But it may be one of the reasons the denominations have become less influential.

We used to have national staff much more visible in the regions interpreting national policies. Before 1970, the staff in the regions were national staff who took their direction mainly from the national boards. Until the 1960s, Conference Executive Secretaries were volunteers.

Then the Conferences were given block grants to use as they chose. They could have their own staff. These staff would network with national people of course, but they were directed by the Conferences. All of that really diminished the visibility of those national staff folks.

Alan Barss: I have the impression that the national church focuses on issues, but that at the local level, we focus on people and on worship. Actually, there's a different "flavor" to the people who get involved in Conference and nationally. Different people get involved. They are really interested in wider issues, interested in justice issues on a bigger scale. Often a global scale.

Marion Best: And sometimes their congregations are not much interested in hearing from them and they may have very little involvement in a congregation. I have one friend who tried very hard to tell her congregation what she was involved in nationally. She said, "They don't want to hear from me."

Sometimes, those Conference or national committees become almost like congregations in the sense of being a person's primary support group. That's where they find their church.

At the local congregational level, there's a lot of emphasis on the worship life. Bud Phillips of the Vancouver School of Theology has developed a way of helping congregations look at themselves through what he calls four "windows." One window is the worshiping community. The second might be called the learning community. The third is the supportive servant community focused on pastoral care. And the fourth is action and advocacy.

The congregations I have worked with usually discover that worship and pastoral care are the areas that get most of their money, time, and energy. That includes the time of the professional staff as well as volunteers. Christian Education, including adult education, would be third most of the time. Advocacy has always been at the bottom unless it involves some local issue that people are all steamed up about. For most congregations it's a tiny little corner carried by a few people who get involved in "Ten Days for World

What do you know about groups such as Ten Days for World Development, the Task Force on Corporate Responsibility, etc.?

Is it possible to focus on both people and issues?

How many people in your congregation are interested in what goes on beyond your church's four walls?

Development" or something like that.

So the priorities of the congregations are usually quite different from those of the church at the Conference or national level. I remember we used to say, "First United in Vancouver does our outreach work for us. We pay mission support money for them to do that work." Some people would go and be volunteers there. Some would collect socks and mittens and send them off. But we were not really actively involved in an outreach ministry. We left advocacy work to the Conference and national people.

Then the national people would try to get congregational support, but mostly they didn't get it. And there were often some angry feelings when national leaders or groups spoke out on controversial issues.

How well does that description match your congregation?

Swirling changes

...three things are happening around us simultaneously:

First, our present confusion about mission hides the fact that we are facing a fundamental change in how we understand the mission of the church. Beneath the confusion we are being stretched between a great vision of the past and a new vision that is not yet fully formed.

Second, local congregations are now being challenged to move from a passive, responding role in support of mission to a front-line, active role. The familiar roles of laity, clergy, executive, bishop, church council, and denominational bureaucrat are in profound transition all around us.

Third, institutional structures and forms developed to support one vision of our mission are rapidly collapsing... I believe that we are being called to be midwives for a new church, working to help our present forms and structures give birth to forms appropriate for the new mission of the church.

Loren B. Mead
The Once and Future Church
The Alban Institute, 1991, p.5

A loss of nerve

Faye Wakeling: I see in the national structures a lot of pressure not to **allow** national leaders to speak out on any significant issues. There's a real intention, over the last numbers of years, to control the voice of the church, to be certain that everything we do and say is "representative,"— that authorization goes all the way up the scale from the grassroots and comes all the way back down again before it is said. It may be that the courageous work the church did around the sexuality issue in 1988 has been used as a reason why the church has to be careful. Are people saying the church has had enough conflict—they can't deal with any more?

Jim Sinclair: Well, that's happened in the Roman Catholic Church too. In the March 6, 1994, issue of the *Catholic New*

Times there's an excellent article on stilling the voice of the social action people in Canada. That's not unlike what's happened all through Latin America. The conservatives have been placed in positions of power and they've put the lid on. And we wonder, why is that happening?

Roland Kawano: I think it's somehow tied to the recession.

Marion Best: Is it a response to anxiety? Any time it feels as if things are getting out of control and there's chaos in the world as well as in the church, the first reaction is to become more bureaucratic and have more rules.

I'm concerned about the bureaucracy that we seem to be developing as a church. We seem to be trying to keep everything orderly and under control.

Should those who put the money on the plate have control over what our national leaders say?

Is there some way the church nationally and the church locally could be more connected?

Church and culture

Phyllis Airhart: Churches aren't simply reacting against their loss of influence in the culture. We're being profoundly affected by the same things that the culture is going through. I think the leaders in our church and the leaders in the government might have a good time talking to each other. Despite their very different political assumptions, I think they are dealing with some of the same phenomena, not just regionalism but an increasing localism. Things have changed.

Ed Searcy: We wouldn't necessarily want to go back to the days when we had one "man" shows in the United Church. We don't want a Ray Hord or somebody like that to put us all straight and speak for the United Church. We wouldn't trust somebody with

The great divide

What happened religiously [in the 1960s] is much the same as what happened politically. Boomers in the late 1950s and early 1960s were a generation well on their way to a normal respect for the political process: They had high levels of trust in government and felt that political leaders cared about what people thought. But within a span of ten years—from 1963 to 1973—they abandoned their once hopeful outlook for a new course of political independence and institutional separation. By their late teens and early twenties, trust in government plummeted, party loyalty declined and the number of political party "independents" shot up. The analogy to organized religion seems indisputable; greater separation from institutions and corresponding increase in emphasis on individual choice.

Wade Clark Roof
from *A Generation of Seekers*,
Harper San Francisco 1993, p.57

that, just as we wouldn't trust any political leader in that way. We're breathing different air. Or something.

Mardi Tindal: But, as a layperson in my congregation, I count on some help. It really helped me to have General Council's action on Oka. I wrote my MP on that basis knowing I wasn't speaking on my own. I wrote my own letter and I said, "I support my church in this issue." I know I wasn't alone in that.

What's the fine line between "leading" and "shoving it down our throats"?

I would never have written that letter unless General Council had spoken out. I'm happy to get the "Urgent Action" notices from the Hamilton Conference network. I read those and I make my own decisions. Is this something I'm ready to add my voice to? My church has helped me by gathering some information, by giving some criteria for action, by helping me think it through. That's an important part of who I am, connected with this church.

Subtle influence

Marion Best: Alan, earlier you said your dad could have some influence through ministry, but that wouldn't be your route. To what extent do you look to the church for support, or resources or anything, in your ministry in the world of politics?

Alan Barss: Not as much as I should. I don't consciously research what the church would say about this issue, or what Jesus would say about that one, or what the Bible says about any specific subject.

For participants, this was more than an intellectual exercise. Animated conversation continued over meals in the Cedar Glen cafeteria. Marion, Faye, Phyllis, Mardi and Ed ponder the connections of faith and politics.

In the political sphere you don't have time for that kind of study. You just don't have time to develop the reasoned responses. You want to take time reflecting on things and praying about things and researching things. But society doesn't give you that luxury. Especially in politics which is where I work every day.

There's incredible pressure to continually react. We bend to that pressure, sometimes. We've taken a lot of heat for delaying decisions or doing implementation studies because it was more proper to make informed decisions.

But more often than not you have to make quick decisions. And so I rely on my instincts and I work hard on developing those instincts—to tune those to my understanding of what the Christian faith teaches.

Do you think people in political power pay attention when church people send them letters about various issues?

Pamela Brown: There's always a dialogue, a conversation going on between you and the church in various ways. That is part of what you bring to the decisions you're required to make quickly. That's certainly true for me in my medical profession. You know that there's always this sort of background happening so that when you're faced with an ethical decision that has to be made very fast, you do in fact bring all of that religious sensibility to how you respond.

Alan Barss: Very much so.

We're United
Pamela: I wonder if we're all a bit more tentative than we used to be. Especially after 1988 and the shock of the massive exodus from the church and the withholding of money. I wonder if the effects of that go deeper than we really know.

Much as I celebrate the United Church decision on gay ordination, I believe that people are now more likely to tippytoe around even if they believe in something very strongly. "Yes," they'll say, "but we have to watch the budget."

It happens right at the local level. In our church, it was suggested that it would be appropriate to hold a vigil on December 6 to remember the Montreal massacre. But a couple of people leapt to their feet and objected. "Let's not upset anybody." I have the sense that maybe ten years ago we wouldn't have backed off so quickly.

Not the worst thing

The United Church of Canada is the most Canadian of churches, and like Canada, its strengths may be the same as its weaknesses; diversity tolerance, compromise, humility, practicality and niceness. Truth gets written by committee, mystery gets lost in the negotiation, decency gets translated into dullness and the spirit gets hamstrung by the bureaucracy. (Some jocularly call it the "Church of Christ, Sociologist.") "The United Church has an amazing ability to avoid doing the thing that will screw up the works," a Vancouver theologian explained to me. "It may not do the best thing, but it can be counted on not to do the worst."

That may have been reassuring for him, but it did not strike me as much of a rock upon which to build a church.

Ron Graham
God's Dominion
McClelland & Stewart Inc.,
481 University Ave.,
Toronto, ON, M5G 2E9
page 222

Phyllis Airhart: But in a way that is part of being United Church. Ron Graham, in his chapter on the United Church in his book *God's Dominion,* talks about us as being the most Canadian of all denominations, and part of that is our "niceness."

Ed Searcy: The beginning of the century was a time of great optimism. Maybe overblown optimism. It's different at the end of this century. There's an underlying despair about our society and our faith. We need stories about change from our past, how we responded to difficult circumstances.

We were so caught up in our identity. We're United. It was kind of a joyous thing. I remember in our church there were big carved letters *Ut Omnes Unum Sint* "that all may be one." I looked at that every Sunday.

And we saw ourselves as nice people and we didn't do things because they would upset someone. And then came the scandal of realizing we were not who we thought we were. There were headlines every day in the *Globe and Mail.* Our dirty laundry was out there in the *Province* and the *Sun* so everybody could see. That was a major identity crisis we had in 1988.

People would ask, "You're **still** in the United Church?" Sure there were bumper stickers that said, "Proud to be United Church," but they were a reaction to that identity crisis. United Church "pride" has been very fragile ever since.

We've talked about the things that brought us into the church. But our individual stories implied a bunch of questions that all of us here are struggling with. Can we be transformed? What will a new United Church look like? We can't pretend to be quite so "united" anymore. If we ever were.

Would you talk about your membership in the United Church at your office or over the back fence? What would you say if you did?

Maybe that's growing up. Maybe that "united" business was all a mirage. We didn't tell each other what we really felt. Faye, you talked about never discussing faith and sex in your early church experience. Maybe we weren't all that honest with each other.

It hurts at home

Marion Best: The divisiveness when it happens in the congregation is so difficult, isn't it? It was one thing to see it happening at General Council, but those folks don't see each other at the post office every day. When that trust disintegrates in a congregation, it hurts far more than it does in the Presbyteries and Conferences and General Council.

Loren Mead, in his book *The Once And Future Church*, says we're moving away from national denominational structures toward the congregation. I realize how much I have mixed feelings about seeing that go. How many congregations will really engage social consciousness issues if we lose the denominational structure?

Who decides what is important?

We told glowing stories here about our congregations. But some of us said that it wasn't in congregations that they were able to be fed. That's not what raised our social consciousness.

Jim Sinclair: Part of our identity has been that we are a national church. That's important to us. It's important to our history. Now that's fragmenting.

I'll give you an example of how fragmented it is in the congregation. When we were doing some work back in the early 80s around the whole question of homosexuality—this was at our Manitou Conference meeting—we were asked to spend time in prayer overnight considering this question: "Would I give serious consideration or could I agree to have homosexual persons welcomed openly in the church?" And another question was, "Would I agree to have them ordained in the church?"

I remember one woman in our group saying, "If I were answering this question myself, I would be answering in favor of homosexual ordination. But if I want my marriage to survive I have to say no."

So which is more important? Relationships or issues? Or can you separate the two?

We've got issues that tear people apart even within primary relationships. We've had to face that sort of thing in our congregations.

The other thing is the fear of legal action. How many people are tiptoeing around these days because we've had 21 people named in one major lawsuit and 18 named in another?

No matter which way these things play out, people have been wounded. There have been expenses involved.

Part of our identity has been shattered in that respect. The processes of the church are no longer adequate to many of the challenges that are presented to us. External forces are making some decisions for us and about us.

What about our identity in terms of what we believe and the way we articulate our beliefs? That's changing too. In my adult lifetime in the church, those things have never converged the way they have right now. It's almost as if we're in another reformation—with all the exciting and fearful possibilities that offers.

Does church leadership come from the bottom up or from the top down? If you're not a member of Presbytery or a national committee, do you have any say in the United Church?

Loren Mead says the role of the national church will be research and teaching. Okay, but where will the united voice come from to articulate a faith statement or a social position? My sense is that these will have to come out of community groups. We'll have leadership, but it's going to come from the local level up, rather than from the top down.

Marion Best: You are confident about that?

Basic values

Jim Sinclair: I think it's already happening on a very limited basis. I think a lot of it's happening and we haven't recognized it.

People are realizing that there are superordinate values—primary values that are fundamentally important in our church. I think that's part of what we're doing now—trying to name these values that have a "higher commonality" about them. I think some of them are emerging. People are beginning to name them.

Community is one of them.

Marion Pardy: I think our identity as a church is in our openness and inclusiveness. The people on the street expect that when they come off the street to the church office they're going to be greeted with a certain amount of respect.

Is it important to you that you're a member of the United Church?

People in our community, if they want something that's broader than the narrowness of some denominations, tend to approach the United Church. They expect a positive response from us. At the local level, openness and inclusiveness is the image that people have of the United Church.

In Newfoundland, the United Church is the one denomination that has been in support of a unified school system. A lot of that comes from the brave and bold stances of General Council.

But maybe (and I have a lot of fear about this) we need to be losing our identity. Maybe part of the call is to work with people of goodwill in other faith communities, people of goodwill who have no identifiable faith communities, or wherever there are people working for justice and compassion. That might be a community organization or another faith organization.

That makes us, as a church, less visible. We can no longer simply say, "This is the United Church of Canada at work!"

Does the United Church really need to lose its own identity to work effectively with other faith groups and community organizations?

Faye Wakeling: I probably see this a bit more in Quebec because it is such a Catholic province. We're called on so often to be with people in rites of passage, in times of importance in their lives, when they no longer can call on the church they've grown up in. They're Catholic, but sometimes, because of divorce, they've left that church and have no other place they can go. And yet at different times in their lives—be it birth, be it death, be it marriage—they're looking for something that will help them name the reality of what they're living in the face of God. But they can't do it in their own tradition. Especially some of the young people who have no background in a faith tradition. They're looking for some help in moving through those important times in their lives. So our church is often seen as a place where people can come and ask for that.

Do you look to the United Church to help you through the important times in your life?

That scares some people because they feel we haven't got any guidelines. We'll marry anybody, bury anybody. But I think we're being challenged to let go of some denominational identity so that we can minister to that necessity.

A "liberal" church
Marion Best: Phyllis said she had studied her way into the United Church. I think many of us have appreciated the intellectual openness we found here. I came asking questions and I wasn't turned away.

Ed Searcy: Sometimes yes, sometimes no. Often at conferences and meetings, you can be excluded by the people who talk about inclusiveness if your theology is too far to the left or to the right. If you can't buy our line, then we're going to have to set up a covenant community so we can be clear who's in, right? We're going

The Gospel distorted

We have come to see that this [attempt to translate the Gospel into theological principles], though well intentioned, is misguided. The theology of translation assumes that there is some kernel of *real* Christianity, some abstract essence that can be preserved even while changing some of the old Near Eastern labels. Yet such a view distorts the nature of Christianity. In Jesus we meet not a presentation of basic ideas about God, world, and humanity, but an invitation to join up, to become part of a movement, a people. By the very act of our modern theological attempts at translation, we have unconsciously distorted the gospel and transformed it into something it never claimed to be—ideas abstracted from Jesus, rather than Jesus and his people.

Stanley Hauerwas and William H. Willimon,
Resident Aliens
Abingdon Press, 1989. p.21

to have to set up a women's network over here, and if you speak out against it over there, then you are excluded from our inclusive community.

Old-fashioned liberalism, which was very much a part of our early United Church ethos, said you didn't need to be afraid of asking questions, of allowing the tradition to critique new ideas and new ideas to critique the tradition. I have felt very alone in some places when I have raised a question, in all honesty thinking that I was allowed to do so in the United Church, and then been slotted by somebody into an opposing camp for life.

I experience that less at the congregational level than at Presbytery and Conference. I had experiences with the farmers in

Do you get strange looks when you ask certain kinds of questions?

the Prairies and with the suburban people in Richmond that were far more inclusive than with the people who use that word at regional and national events.

Marion Best: So when we talk about inclusiveness we're not necessarily being inclusive?

Ed Searcy: Sometimes very exclusive.

Are we in a period of backlash against some of the movements that have swept our society and our church?

Pamela Brown: Last night, a colleague and I did a presentation on violence in the family. When the question came up about abused men, it seemed as if it was not okay to ask about that or discuss it. Is that the sort of thing you're talking about?

Ed Searcy: For a man, for example, to dare to critique feminist theology is very difficult. I understand that. There were too many times women simply heard the knee-jerk reaction of a guy who didn't want to hear what they were saying. At the other end of the spectrum, in conservative circles, you have to be very careful that you're not slotted into a particular camp because the kinds of questions you ask might imply some credence for liberal ideologies.

Permeable boundaries

Phyllis Airhart: There is both left-wing and right-wing fundamentalism in a lot of mainstream churches. There are invisible boundaries and you bump into them without ever seeing them.

I think that what the United Church has tended to have, at least in the past, is more permeable boundaries than a lot of other denominations.

It's the vision of permeable boundaries that I'd like to think we have. If we operate with the assumption that there are no boundaries, I think we delude ourselves. It's like the question of power. We can claim we're all egalitarian and that we're not going to have structures. But sometimes those non-hierarchical groups are the most manipulative because the people who do the leading or manipulating are not named and hence not accountable.

Alan Barss: I like the idea of permeable boundaries. The boundaries are there, but I have some ability to affect them. People like to know they can make a difference to how the church thinks, and I think that's true in the United Church.

As I did my research before coming to this meeting, I had some people who described the United Church as very "liberal" and others who described it as "conservative." The people who said it was "liberal" were, for the most part, men. The ones who said it was "conservative" were mostly women. Is that really a gender thing, or was that accidental?

Do you experience the United Church as "liberal" or "conservative" on women's issues? Which group would you consider yourself and your friends to be in?

Pamela Brown: I don't think it's accidental. I think women experience the church as very conservative because it has been very slow to recognize and celebrate the many initiatives and gifts that women offer. I don't think that's been the experience of men. Their gifts and offerings have been welcomed and celebrated in the church, which therefore might feel quite liberal to them.

Faye Wakeling: I think if we're talking about the identity of our church we have to say that the role of women has been very significant throughout our history and has become increasingly so. Women are producing a lot of the challenge and unease that's

How has the changing role of women affected your congregation?

going on now and it's not just around issues of sexuality. We're challenging the church to recognize that women's experiences and gifts are crucial. I don't think we really know how significant that role has been.

Ed Searcy: Look at any congregation. Look at the people each Sunday morning in church. Most of them are women. Look at my Bible study group. I've got 25 women and 6 men. Why doesn't the church speak to men?

Why doesn't the church speak to men?

And yet it's been very male dominated. Male clergy and male leaders. The male clergy are still there but the leadership is now mostly women. It's sad that, for some reason, what we are about doesn't say anything to men.

Alan Barss: But I still see men exerting their influence through the power structures.

The age shift
Ed Searcy: The real question of our United Church identity is the shift in the age of our leadership. The leaders are recycled and recycled and recycled. They have chaired the board three times already, are back for another time, and now are 65.

Phyllis Airhart: Both my husband, Matthew, and I were asked to be on the nominating committee at our church. We were the youngest members there. We laughed afterwards and Matthew said, "Gee, I felt weird being there. Why did we get asked? There must be people who have been in the church for years and years and who know people better."

I said, "That's precisely why we've been asked, so that when we get to that age we'll know how to do it."

Mardi Tindal: We're going to have to talk about our identity in relation to youth. Many of us here talked about how the church nurtured and educated us. I look at my kids and the staff at the camp and I'm thrilled to say they're very excited about being identified with a church that cares about the important issues like the environment. Probably that's at the head of their list. They're glad that the United Church at least cares about these things.

But most of them are not really active in our congregations. Or they're just holding on by a thread. Those that **are** involved in youth ministry, networks, youth forums and stuff like that, are only a small proportion of that next generation, and we're only holding them by a thread.

Marion Best: There isn't anybody in this room who didn't have some significant interaction with a church before they were adults. We weren't all United Church, but everybody here either was born into the United Church or had some significant interaction in another Christian community.

But it's quite evident that the church is no longer the primary community for children. There was a time when the church was the social center, where you went for your community. There are so many more options now, and there is so much more money, and people are able to do other things.

I can remember the first time a theater opened on a Sunday. In the former times, there never would have been ball games or practices or anything like that on Sunday morning. Sunday morning was kept set apart.

Now, families who want to be involved in the church have to make really tough choices: "Am I going to teach Sunday school or am I going to take my kid to hockey practice."

Ed Searcy: Adults who became involved in the church in the last few years arrived with a blank slate.

We don't have an identity that helps us know how to bring people in. People come in and they ask questions like, "What's a church?"

"I came with a friend," they tell me, "and now I've discovered I keep coming here on my own. I'm not sure why. Can you tell my why? What is this place all about?"

People are surprised to wind up in a church when they've never really been in a church before. It's wonderful and hopeful, but it's quite new to our ethos. Being Canadian and being United Church were almost the same thing. You loved it or you hated it, but you stayed with it because that's what everybody did. But now it is no longer "normal" to be part of any church, especially the United Church.

Phyllis Airhart: There are a lot of women in the church, older women whose identity of being United Church means being caught up in the service to the church. But now, women are working out-

Is it possible to have one congregation that meets the needs of both the young people and the older folks? Do we need two kinds of services?

How much support do you get in your family if you choose church over hockey practice?

What keeps you involved? Why do you belong to this United Church congregation?

side the home and they don't have time to volunteer in the same way.

We haven't faced up to the reality of women working outside the home and the impact that this has on congregational life. I'm an example of this myself.

Our church had to give up doing Meals on Wheels because there just weren't people to do it any longer. I found myself explaining that I couldn't do Meals on Wheels because I was teaching. One guy got quite annoyed with me.

"Yes," he said, "but you **chose** to do that. If you really wanted to do Meals on Wheels you would stop working."

Ed Searcy: One of the things about our tradition that seems to be holding firm is our United Church creed: "We are not alone..." It shows up in World Council of Churches books and in publications all over the world.

I think, congregationally, people consider the United Church creed and it seems to work for them. It picked up our ethos and our tradition and tried to restate things that we couldn't say.

A statement of intention

We wish to stand within the United Church of Canada, which we understand to be:
• a community of people who follow the teachings of Jesus
• a community that is open and accepting of all peoples
• a community that is continually learning, exploring and struggling to understand and express their beliefs
• a community which offers and encourages time for reflection
• a community that reaches out in love and service to others
• a community that acknowledges a variety of beliefs, encourages dialogue and challenges us to grow.

The Enquiry Class of 1994
First United Church
Kelowna, B.C.
(used by permission)

Mardi Tindal: It's the one thing I've made sure my children know. We say it as a grace at meals because I really want them to know it.

Phyllis Airhart: The creed sounds sort of '60ish to me. The language doesn't have the mystery or majesty of the Apostolic creed.

It really is a very complex question, isn't it—this matter of who we are as a United Church, whether we're talking nationally or in our own congregations? It's my hope the conversation we started at Cedar Glen will be continued in your own congregation.

Talking about who we are and what is important to us provides us with valuable data on which to make decisions about our future.

A New Creed

We are not alone, we live in God"s World.
We believe in God
who has created and is creating,
who has come in Jesus
the Word made flesh,
to reconcile and make new,
Who works in us and others by the Spirit.

We trust in God.
We are called to be the Church,
to celebrate God's presence,
to love and serve others,
to seek justice and resist evil,
to proclaim Jesus, crucified and risen,
our judge and our hope.

In life, in death, in life beyond death,
God is with us.
We are not alone.
Thanks be to God.

© by permission of the United Church of Canada

For group discussion:
What are the priorities in your congregation? Where do you put the most time and money?
What gets people energized in your congregation? What do they really support and what do they ignore?
What is the mission of your congregation?

CHAPTER 4

Potholes and pathways

Even after all that discussion, we still had trouble getting a handle on who we were and what we should become. For the most part, we resisted the temptation to point to our leadership, whether lay or clergy, and say, "They are the problem!"

So we talked about some of the problems we face and about our structures and how those could be more responsive. There seem to be fewer lay people able to give substantial time to the church. And yet there is a general awareness, reflected in surveys and comments made by many people, of a deep spiritual hunger.

In many congregations, budget cuts have meant fewer paid, professional staff. In the area where I live, one of the larger congregations is down from two clergy to one. Another congregation has moved from a having a full-time clergy person, to having one only part-time.

*That's both frightening and disturbing. And yet there is an element of hope in it. It seems to me we need to ask the question, "What kind of work, or which area, should our leaders be focusing on?" That invites a lot of questions, such as, what is most important? What are our priorities? And what should we **stop** trying to do or be?*

It takes courage to ask those kinds of questions.

Faye Wakeling, Pamela Brown, and Jim Sinclair struggle with the questions: "What's holding us? Who's calling us? And to what?"

Marion Best: Maybe we should begin with a list of all the things that we don't want to lose. Both Jim and Phyllis said, "I really love my congregation." Let's hear about congregations that seem to be life-giving.

Pamela Brown: Yours too, Marion. You said the same about your own little church community in Naramata.

What is life-giving about your congregation? What don't you want to lose?

Ed Searcy: Faye was talking about people who have found their life in places other than the conventional church, such as in that Bible study group with the women in poverty. There are other forms of church that are life giving—St. Columba House for instance.

Pathways

Jim Sinclair: The University of Mexico didn't put any sidewalks into their new campus for a year. Then they put the sidewalks where people had worn the paths.

What pathways already exist for us? Where are the signs of activity, of life in our congregations?

Then if we looked at the church from the air, so to speak, we'd know what's left off at the sides. We wouldn't put sidewalks where nobody walks. I think people have already made decisions and we, the leaders in the church, are trying to name them.

It reminds me of a remark Gandhi made to some reporters. A large group of people he was traveling with began to move away from where he was being interviewed. He said, "There go my people. I must follow, for I am their leader."

Marion Best: Well, let's name some of those paths.

In the congregation I attend there's a group which chooses to meet at 9:00 a.m. with adults and children together. I think it's significant that the minister and his family also attend this group. They take their turn leading once a month and they're participants the rest of the time.

I know another congregation that tried it. They didn't have

Take risks

Many community members have become much more conscious than 10 or 15 years ago of the urgency to do something drastic. They now realize clearly that by continuing on their current course, communities are simply headed for gradual extinction. Therefore, they are prepared to try something and to take risks. This consciousness is an asset to be emphasized.

Assembly of Quebec Bishops, 1992 p.26

Do you feel comfortable with Gandhi's kind of leadership, or do you want a leader who is more assertive? Why?

Present tense credibility

Whenever the presence and influence of any organization or institution is in decline in a culture, great care must be taken to ensure a promising future. In human terms, when the church was center stage in Canadian society, it could afford to be complacent and even somewhat presumptuous. Being in a position of strength meant that errors in judgment or absence of deliberate strategies were not especially consequential. The 1990s do not afford such past luxuries.

At this stage in the history of the church in Canada, faith communities have to work harder and be more strategic simply to maintain present levels of attendance. Because the majority of Canadians are no longer involved in church life, internal integrity will of necessity have to accompany any aspirations for external influence.

The practices of the people of God will have to coincide with the proclaimed church dogma. The people who go to church will need to be the visible church in the world during the week. Keeping the church building in good repair and visible in the community will not be enough. Nor will a church's rich history and positive reputation in the neighborhood be enough to keep new people coming. Rather than depending on contributions of the past, the church of the future will have to carve out a present-tense credibility. And should it be any other way?

Donald C. Posterski and Irwin Barker, from *Where's a Good Church?*

How important is the community life of the church to you?

any music resources, they didn't have any professional staff person, and after a while the people just couldn't maintain it. The rest of the congregation complained about the fact that these people weren't in the "regular" service. So those folks lost heart. Some went back into the regular congregational life. Some just didn't go anywhere.

Ed Searcy: One congregation that I was at had a service that usually went from 9:30 a.m. until about 10:45. The second service started at 11:00.

Some of those who came to the later service got frustrated because there was nowhere to park and the narthex was packed. So they said, "For six months, let's try coming at 11:15 to give a half-hour break."

But within six weeks they were really unhappy. They realized how important all that crowded time was—they felt like one community and they enjoyed all those children. Finally they realized the best thing was to have a really crowded narthex and nowhere to put their coats and nowhere to park their cars because that's how it had to be. They found out what was really important and then put up with the rest.

The congregation that I'm at now sometimes wishes it had those problems.

Nuts and bolts

Marion Pardy: What makes a situation life-giving? How do you know?

Jim Sinclair: A good question to ask in that regard, Marion, is: "Who takes out the garbage? Who gets the dirty jobs?"

Who takes out the garbage— who does the dirty jobs— in your congregation?

Ed Searcy: Yeah—the nuts and bolts of a covenant community. How hospitable is the church to different communities of people? It's necessary to name those particular nuts and bolts issues. If the community changes to make it hospitable for one group, then it may feel less familiar for the community that's always been there.

Roland Kawano: I went to a church in Fullerton, California. At the first service they had 2,500 people, and the same number at the second. I wondered, how does this work? Why do people come? Could it be that the pastor kept talking about the forgiveness of sins? People just kept pouring in and someone would stand up and ask us to squeeze and we'd all squeeze to get in one more person. They had all the nuts and bolts worked out, even a team of young people on roller blades to supervise the parking.

Obviously not a United Church. But why not?

Faye Wakeling: I sense we're looking for ways in which the church can support the work and ministry that people are engaged in. It is like the base communities in Latin America that gather because they have something they are trying to work with and be faithful with. They want the presence of the church to be with them, to move along beside them—not to direct them or to take them over.

While Pam hangs a sheet of newsprint recording significant points on the wall, Marion Pardy and Phyllis Airhart continue to focus on the discussion

And we see lots of different groups like that. I hear of people working in hospitals as chaplains—who already have a horrendous job trying to meet the needs of patients and families. These chaplains are getting more and more requests to become a pastoral community with the doctors or nurses who are dealing with the very complex ethical problems around AIDS and kidney transplants and so on.

We hate making tough decisions because somebody always gets hurt. But do we have any alternative?

Roland Kawano: So we face the triage question. What do we cut? What do we stop doing? I don't like to talk about triage, because someone else does it, never the wounded one. Someone else makes the decision, not the people who are affected. Who is going to survive and who isn't?

Marion Best: That's why we've come together to talk about the future of our church, so that we get to decide those things for ourselves. If we just sit around and wait and keep doing the same things, in the end somebody else decides.

Small groups

Mardi Tindal: I think one of the most important ingredients is life-giving worship. In my own congregation, within the excellent preaching and within the excellent liturgy, people are invited to think about the issues in their lives in a new light, things such as health issues and value issues.

Then invitations are made and it's up to us in the pews to say, "That's something I'd like to talk with some others about and do something about."

The United Church has been a program-driven church for so long that we expect clergy and paid staff to organize programs, programs which we may not be able to afford to do any longer. Laypeople need to feel their own strength so we can take the initiative as members of a congregation to say, "This is what I want to meet with other people about."

Do you wait for others to take leadership? Is it because you don't know how? Or are you just scared?

I think the challenge is to liberate and strengthen people to take that kind of initiative on their own. Perhaps you're a nurse dealing with a certain kind of problem. Well, find out where the other faithful people are who can help you in this discussion.

One of the great things about the ministry of *Spirit Connection* is that we go around tapping people on the shoulder and saying, "You're doing something really wonderful here."

They look surprised. "We are?"

"Yes," we say. "Tell me what you're doing. And tell me why you're doing it." In the telling they really articulate the deep roots of their convictions and their actions. But often they don't realize those convictions and those roots until we ask.

For me worship is so critical. In worship, people are strengthened to make those connections, to create those affiliations, to respond to their colleagues who are going through ethical dilemmas, and to affirm and celebrate the ministry that is happening in far more places than we realize.

Phyllis Airhart: One of the things that makes congregations feel discouraged is that many of the older forms of community within congregations, forms that also tied one congregation with another, are changing. Like the UCW and the AOTS.

When I look at the reduction in the numbers of UCW units, it feels very discouraging. And when you're discouraged, it's easy not to see the other types of community that form in a congregation. Women may be involved in very different ways in various congregations. It may be a Bible study group like Marion's, or a group engaged in some aspect of social justice work. Often this happens more in those several hours they're spending at church on Sunday.

One of the changes is that people tend far more to ask, "What's in this for me personally?" We still operate on the assumption that it's the church's need or the need of mission that brings people into a group. That isn't nearly as true anymore.

Alan Barss: When I think "community" in my congregation, it's those people who are involved in my small social justice group—only eight or ten couples—that I feel close to. Not the other 150 people who sit in church every Sunday.

The other closeness I felt was in the choir. Again a small group

On the right track

At one time, theologians argued that the chief purpose of humankind was to glorify God. Now it would seem that the logic has been reversed: the chief purpose of God is to glorify humankind. Spirituality no longer is true or good because it meets absolute standards of truth or goodness but because it helps me get along. We are the judge of its worth. If it helps me find a vacant parking space I know my spirituality is on the right track.

Robert Wuthnow
from *Sharing the Journey*
The Free Press, 1994. p. 18

Does that mean we've got to "market" the church, so that people can see the benefits available for them?

who met regularly, who shared in music, song, and laughter.

All those committees

Why can't we just not do something, if there aren't enough people to do it? Can we leave some things undone so we can do essential things better?

Ed Searcy: I think the bureaucratic structure of the church is causing us to work, work, work, work and so we're not able to get at forming small life-giving groups.

We've typically modeled our congregational structures after the General Council and the Conference levels so that we have about 12 committees that we struggle like mad to fill. The work is important, and it's hard to figure out how you could **not** have all those committees. Sometimes they function as small groups, but more often than not you do the work and then you go home. There's no energy left over to be part of a small group where you can experience some community.

Yet it does happen, but often not for those people who put all their energy into committees. There's the quilters' group in my congregation where quilting is secondary to all the other stuff that goes on. And the choir, and the seniors, the Friday Friends community, and the youth group.

One of my frustrations, as the paid staff person, is that I'm so caught up in maintaining all that bureaucratic structure—in attending meetings—that there's little time to be a minister. And I wonder if part of letting go is to move back to a simpler structure.

Alan Barss: That's a really good point. When I talked to people before coming to this event, many of them complained about how busy they were, how many activities they were involved in.

If you create a bureaucratic structure which, by its nature, draws the committed people in your congregation, then it also keeps them out of life-giving activities of the con-

Actions vs. words

The rhetoric from the pulpit urges engagement with the world and defines one's "real" ministry as job, community life, family, etc., all of which takes place *outside* the church. Yet the bulletin, the parish organization, the pastor, and staff urge and reward engagement with parish *activities.* Ministry outside the church is rarely recognized and never rewarded. Ministry inside *is* recognized and rewarded. The pastoral calling that is done is generally done in homes, not in the workplace. Assignments to responsibilities in the congregation are generally made according to the congregation's organizational needs, not the expertise of the lay person. What is *said* at church undergirds the [new understanding of the church]. What is *done* tends to reflect assumptions left over from the [old understanding].

Loren B. Mead
The Once and Future Church
The Alban Institute, 1991, p.35

gregation. They're just too busy. They're too tired. They just can't get involved in a Kerygma Bible study session, or a social outreach group, or just a night of friendship to recharge their batteries. So eventually they burn out or leave.

Phyllis Airhart: It's important to invite and support those types of small groups. But remember that for many people the work of the committees has been their way of becoming involved in the work of the church.

My husband, Matthew, for example. His involvement in the church took on new life when he was asked to be on the pastoral relations committee. He began to see the life of the church in a completely different way and has been much more interested.

He's not simply doing it out of a sense of duty. It's because he cares about the church. If we replace those committees we have to provide a variety of other ways that people can be involved in the church.

Spiritual structures

Alan Barss: It may not mean replacing the committees. It may be a new way of functioning within those committees. For instance, I've had some connection with a church that has a council meeting once a month. It's a long meeting, four hours or more. But after a general meeting of half an hour or so, they break off into their committees.

They have **all** their committee meetings that night. Then they come back after an hour and a half or two hours and report back to council, which is a conglomeration of the committees. One night a month—all their committee work—all their council work.

Phyllis Airhart: What if you're on two committees?

Alan Barss: You **can't** be on two committees. Which is a blessing and a curse. That's the trade off. But it's a lot easier to recruit people and get people involved and it doesn't tie them up.

On the other hand, our minister at St. James, in Regina, goes to committee meetings every night of the week, every week of the month, because they all meet separately on different nights.

Faye Wakeling: Perhaps we should shift the emphasis from a structural question to a theological question, so that these committees

Do you know how your minister feels about your congregational structure and all those committees?

Are committees always a bad thing? What makes them valuable? What makes them a problem?

Could that system work in your congregation? Would the idea be rejected without ever trying it?

become communities.

They're communities in which you find your spirituality as it is rooted in the work you're doing together. You find your worship together in that group, and you discover the holistic nature of what it means to be church and to be in mission.

Phyllis Airhart: I think a lot of committees have either lost their purpose, or never really knew why they were important in the first place. Such committees are bound to fail.

Marion Pardy: I want to affirm the idea of the committee as the spiritual base of the local congregation. It's not so much that the finance and property committees and others attract the hard-nosed people; it's just that this is the side of us we utilize when we're on those committees. But they can be something more than that.

What do "spirituality" and "ministry" mean to you?

We all know that on the worship committee spiritual growth can take place. It's easy to see worship as ministry. It's not so easy to see the bare facts and figures and questions like, "Who's going to take out the garbage?" as part of ministry. And yet that **is** ministry. We need to find a way of seeing it that way and making committee work a spiritual exercise.

Changing attitudes

Your parents probably talked about "duty." But we hardly use that word any more. Why?

Mardi Tindal: I'd like to think that could happen but I really don't have a lot of hope. As a church, we're incredibly institutional, bureaucratic, organized, and corporate. Our structure, our organization is based on the culture of the over-50s generation, which puts a very high value on saying, "I'll do my duty and I'll invest my time, not because I want to, but because it is my duty and I will feel guilty if I don't do this."

Does "spirituality" mean a hunger for "something more"?

But my under-50 friends aren't inclined to go to a church where they're going to have to be on a committee. They want very badly to go to church and to be nurtured spiritually. They have a spiritual hunger, and they know it. They want to connect with other people who've lost their job, or who have a special-needs child.

People want more than just to keep the institutional wheels humming. At least people my age. People used to compete to go to General Council. It was considered an honor and a privilege. I am told that a couple of weeks ago, at Halton Presbytery, they had to ask for **volunteers** to go to General Council.

Marion Pardy: Do we need to completely reorganize and not have committees at all? How does that financial work get attention if people like you and others say, "No, I don't want that"?

Marion Best: Two-thirds of United Church congregations have fewer than 150 people. When you look at the structure that's expected of a small congregation, you ask yourself how they have enough people to do all that. Nobody would ever get a rest. People work on committees for which they don't have a lot of interest.

I know of one congregation that did something similar to the one you were describing, Alan. They recruited people based on their expertise and their interest. I was talking to them recently and the minister said, "We used to have trouble getting the committees to function. Now the committees are running great, but nobody wants to come to council meetings!"

Maybe a congregation could develop a committee structure or small group structure based on people's interests. If you have three or more people interested in something, they become a committee to do that or to talk about that. If you don't have anybody who wants to do a newsletter, then you don't do a newsletter. Or flowers in the chancel. Or whatever.

I think of one congregation where a woman had worked with the junior choir for years and years. She said, "I'd really like to give this up, but I don't want to disappoint the children, and if I give it up, there's nobody who wants to do it." I said, "Just give it up. If people think it is worthwhile, something will happen." Two young women have taken it over.

Alan Barss: She had to be ready to risk allowing the choir to die.

Marion Best: Yes, it meant taking a risk. And that was hard. She struggled for a full two years before she was able to do that. It's a profound theological struggle, you know. Something must die so that another thing can be born.

Mardi Tindal: That's the crisis we're in. I don't have an answer. I know that what we've been doing isn't working any more. People don't want to serve the institution. But that's all they feel they've been asked to do. They're not prepared to put their energies there. That's not where they feel called.

When older folks give up a job, they may feel they are giving up a part of their life, their worthwhileness. Can you expect them to do that easily?

What in your life do you have to let die?

Ed Searcy: Lots of Christian communities through the ages have functioned without committees. Committees are not essential. They're not biblical. Committees are a cultural model that we've adopted from the world around us.

Part of the vision of a life-giving church involves focusing energy on the formation of Christian community, whether that's in small groups or large groups.

That means helping people understand what it means to be a Christian, as opposed to just being a Canadian. How is the church the same as the culture around us, and how is it radically different? In the past there's not been much difference. We've been a little more socially active than the rest of society, but beyond that, as the Gallup poll says, you can tell little difference between mainline Christians and Canadians in general.

Is there really no difference between Christians and other Canadians?

I think we need to bring the concept of "eldership" back. The native community reminds us of this. It has to do with a community of young and old elders, men and women, who take on the responsibility in a shared way of creating a Christian community in this place. I'm talking about a United Church Christian community that takes responsibility for membership, for discipline when dysfunctional things happen. We haven't done that very well.

We are becoming a minority in this culture. But we really haven't come to terms with how minorities survive. We survive by paying more attention to those things that feed and build our community and help it with a sense of identity.

Marion Best: I like the concept of eldership, but I have to be careful because I can easily get too romantic about it. Then I attribute things to the eldership that may not be realistic. Eldership has to do with wisdom and knowledge and experience. I remember being quite shocked as a young person when I found out that some of the older people knew less about the Bible than I did.

Do we have to throw out everything that is old and use only the new stuff? What if you like the traditional things?

But I'm talking about people who are steeped in the faith. These are the wise people. We're going to have fewer and fewer of those folks, because, I think, we've almost lost a generation in the church. People between 35 and 55 are pretty much missing in most of our congregations.

We've got some young families coming and we've got lots of people over 55 and even more over 65. At least where I live, we have. The new church development congregations are an exception. They often have very few people in the over-50 age range.

The mission

Faye Wakeling: I'm getting uncomfortable. I have the feeling that we are turning in on ourselves.

We've talked about the fact that we don't look any different than the rest of society. A lot of that is because we're not. We can't see life from the perspective of those who are not us. But if you sit with aboriginal people or with people who are unemployed, or with women in poverty, you can't help critiquing everything that goes on around us. You look for different answers because none of it's working.

I'm feeling a sense of frustration, because we seem to want to restructure this solid little group so that we can keep this solid little group going, so that this solid little group can know what its faith is about, so that we can bring more people into it. I have a sense we're missing a crisis that's out there.

I'm not even certain the transmission of values can happen there. So where is it going to happen? Where is the potential for that to happen?

The news is full of things the church can or should do something about. Is our own shop really all that we can deal with?

Ed Searcy: You're right. If the church is just an inward focused group, it has no value. But the most active and committed people in the Christian community do have a different set of values and do make a difference in social issues. So I'm talking about increasing the size and the strength of that committed community.

Faye Wakeling: I don't think it happens that way.

Marion Best: If, in fact, the mission of the church is not overseas but in the neighborhood, what does that mean for the kind of work we need to do? And what kind of leadership does it require?

One of the things that's changing the style of leadership in our church is the number of female clergy. They often bring a very different style.

Most women, I think, want to be "connectional." They want to interrelate. I don't know many women who want to fly solo. I shouldn't generalize, because not all women have families. But when I think of what I spent my life doing for 15 years, it was literally running a household. So I had to think, "How do I involve everybody? How do we share responsibility here? How do we build respect for different people's needs? How do we use our resources? We've only got so much money. Does it go for music

Do we have to choose between a "male" leadership style and a "female" style?

lessons or a new dress?" I didn't make those decisions by myself. Most of my life I needed to involve other people.

But I have to be careful not to generalize about that, and I don't want to stereotype. Women have many different styles of leadership.

Journey inward—journey outward
Jim Sinclair: A woman who brought a very different style of leadership and who has influenced me greatly is Elizabeth O'Connor. She was at the Church of the Savior in Washington, DC. I never really knew anything about her until I read *Fortune* magazine one day. They ran a story about an architect who had revitalized an area within Washington, the slums behind the Capitol buildings.

He was a person of conscience looking for meaning. He found his way to the Church of the Savior. Apparently when you go to the Church of the Savior and you say, "I'd like to consider membership," they reply, "We'd be delighted to put you on our waiting list." That's a little different than in my church.

Then you commit to a process called "the journey inward and the journey outward." Elizabeth O'Connor wrote a book with that title.

This architect was mentored by a spiritual elder. They spent time discovering what it was to be "of the church," what it was to be a faithful person, and what it was to have particular gifts.

Then they began the journey outward. Where do your gifts fit? They will suggest ways in which you can act out your

Religion works
Gallup research has found that people with religious affiliations usually are very active in social, charitable and civic activities—through actions such as feeding the hungry, housing the homeless, caring for the sick, educating the young, providing child care and elder care. Indeed the activity of the churched is three times more than those with no formal religious ties. In most communities members of churches and synagogues are the major providers of human services, outspending all corporations and foundations combined by a margin of two to one.

Research gathered from Gallup, the Lilly Endowment, the Independent Sector, and other groups showed that Americans who worship together generally are more likely to reject drugs, to demonstrate literacy, to be more productive in the workplace, and to show commitment to children and family life at levels well above the national average. Equally important, they contribute more than $19 billion annually to other-than-religious human services. This is more than twice the amount contributed by all corporations and foundations. In addition, the dollar value of volunteer time members give to community services is estimated to be more than $6.3 billion annually.

from *Emerging Trends*, Vol. 12, No. 5, the Princeton Religion Research Center.

gifts—coffee house ministry, their church farm retreat program—stuff like that.

But this architect concluded (and apparently this happens quite often) that his particular gift couldn't be slotted within the normal activity of the church. He concluded that his gift was his vocation. He was an architect.

So then the church asks, "How can we as a faithful community help you use your gift?" And he began to ask, "What are the needs within the city that could be addressed by my gift?"

Well, some of the worst slums in the world are located within sight of the Capitol. So he formed a corporation, along with other members of the Church of the Savior, and arranged for some government housing funding.

They relocated the people from the slums, then hired them for the project. All of them were unemployed, the poorest of the poor. They rebuilt the buildings. Then they were given their apartments back, and their rent money went to purchasing their unit. In the process, they'd been trained in various skills.

The Church of the Savior seemed to have the capacity, not to shape a person in its image, but to help the image of that person reshape the church so the church really became a reflection of God.

That has implications for the kind of leaders we choose. It has implications for our church structures. It has real implications for how we see our mission.

What are your particular gifts? How do you discover them? How do you use them?

What is a church?

Faye Wakeling: We seem to use the word "church" interchangeably with "congregation" all the time. I'm still even uneasy with "organized church." Church also exists in places that are not within the formal structure of the church.

Ed Searcy: I need some help to understand what you mean by church "out there." What does it look like? What would be the ingredient that would mean it was Christian community, as opposed to a gathering of like-minded people wanting to do good work?

Faye Wakeling: For me a church is a place that needs to be built and encouraged and nurtured and given resources. Part of the hurtfulness is being involved in the margins of our church. Our church recognizes who we are at St. Columba House and what we are

What is your definition of "church"? Is it the same as a "congregation"?

doing, but doesn't validate it by calling it real church. There's a lot of hurt in people who are in pastoral care, people who are in outreach ministry, people who are in all these peripheral things that are considered important, but who are never seen as the central, pivotal point of what the church is about.

Ed Searcy: I feel really uncomfortable about naming a public space as church. I expect God to be working there, don't get me wrong. But if those people don't think of themselves as "church" then I don't think I have a right to describe them that way.

Marion Pardy: I see a difference between the church as the gathered community and the church as the dispersed community.

When we are the gathered community, we do all of those things that the gathered community does. We worship, we get together in learning groups, we do all those things we would want to name as the Christian church.

What do you need from your church as a gathered community? As a dispersed community?

But when we disperse, when we are commissioned and blessed, we go out into the community as individuals with a sense of belonging to a core group that's strengthening us, helping us to do God's work. Most often that is not named publicly.

Pamela Brown: I think Faye is inviting us to name it as a way of demonstrating and connecting church with folks whose experience with church hitherto was not positive. And it feels important to me.

Marion Pardy: I don't have a problem with naming it when it's appropriate to do so. But sometimes to name it would be to destroy it.

Naming the stages
Marion Best: Many congregations in the United Church face significant difficulties and need to take a careful look at where they are and where they are going.

The culture of the congregation changes, sometimes because of factors that the congregation can do nothing about, such as when the ethnic and racial mix of a community changes.

The thing I hear most often from people in congregations is that they'd like to see more young people in the church. But when young people come they will want to change the culture of the congregation. And then the people who have been there for a long time don't feel so comfortable about it, and resist the initiatives the young people propose. So they want change, but they don't want it badly enough to do what is necessary to effect change.

When a congregation becomes aware of change, or the need to change, for whatever reason, it goes through the same kind of grief process that we go through when we have a significant loss in our personal life.

Denial comes first. "This problem in our church is just a blip." "We could get new people if we had a young minister who could really preach." We deny the reality and simply refuse to deal with it.

Another stage is **bargaining.** Often congregations will bring in someone from outside, "to help us figure out how to fix the problem." But what we really mean is, "Help us to be the way we were." "Fix it" really means to make everything the way we remember it. And of course, that never works.

And so we move to **anger.** People start blaming one another. Or they blame the Presbytery. Or they blame the national church for some policy that is causing all their problems.

A minister, or somebody from the outside called in to help a congregation, really has to understand the roots of the anger, really has to understand the loss and grief and help folks deal with that. Then, when we've dealt with that, we may be ready to acknowledge that we have to transform into something quite different.

The **depression** that comes after anger usually finds us feeling kind of paralyzed and apathetic. We can't make decisions. I worked with one congregation that was pretty well immobilized for two years. They couldn't decide on anything one way or another.

Finally we move to **acceptance**; we realize that we've just got to do something. It may be we've got to join the other congregation and get rid of the one property. It may be we have to put our money into youth or family ministries.

Finally we can look with some clarity at what is really going on and make the right and necessary decision. That decision may be to die creatively, and some churches have done that with great courage and vision. Or the decision may be to move into a new and challenging way of being the church in our community.

What stage is your congregation in? What stage are you in?

Are you personally willing to put some real energy into the future of your church?

Will our church survive?

It's really hard to know whether the illness that a congregation is suffering is terminal, or whether there is a way to reverse the problem. I think it is a matter of asking, "What's the energy level around here? Who will come out to talk about this?" Often that's an indication. Who will come out to more than one meeting to really talk about it? Who will actually be willing to work at this seriously? If you can't get anybody to do that, then I don't know how you can look at creative options.

Sometimes congregations really do have all of the ingredients for viability, but they get into a kind of a funk. Everybody is depressed and there seems to be no energy anywhere. Sometimes that's because the clergy or other leadership have not been given the pastoral care **they** need. We have an epidemic of clergy burn-out, and there is a whole spectrum of reasons for that.

Often it is wise to bring in an outside person from the Presbytery or Conference or one of the United Church continuing education centers. When you yourself are in the unhappy situation, it can be very hard for you to see what is going on, and to help people find a way out of it.

But to start with, it's good to ask some of the right questions, to gather a group together and begin the process of asking intelligent questions and not backing off from the difficult answers they may produce.

How do we describe our church? What makes it go? Where is the leadership? How do the leaders lead?

I'm not just talking about those in formal positions of leadership, like the clergy or the chair

Scratching where they itch

The starting point for proponents of the marketing concept is the consumer. It's where everything begins. Well-worn expressions sum up the outlook. "Find wants and fill them;" "Make what you can sell instead of trying to sell what you can make;" "Love the customer— not the product." In the words of management theorist Peter Drucker, "The aim of marketing is to make selling superfluous. The aim is to know and understand the customer so well that the product fits...and sells itself." Successful organizations in the 1990s know their clientele and know what they are delivering.

What does all this have to do with religion? This: the disparity between Canadians' apparent receptivity to spirituality and their lack of interest in organized religion reveals that the country's religious groups have not done a particularly good job of getting in touch with people's wants and needs. As United Church minister Gordon Turner, the denomination's former head of evangelism and new church development, has put it, "Right now, we're just not scratching where they're itching."

Reginald W. Bibby,
Unknown Gods
Stoddard Publishing, 1993. p.222

of the board. I'm talking about those people who exercise all kinds of informal leadership. Some of that informal leadership is really life-giving, and some of it is destructive.

What kind of a future is God calling us toward?

Who might you bring together for this kind of conversation?

For group discussion:

What is life-giving in your congregation?

What things need to die before you, as a congregation, can move together into the future?

Do you really meet the needs of your people, or do the people serve the needs of the congregation?

How can you discern your own gifts and the gifts of the whole church?

CHAPTER 5

Searching the scriptures

Alan Barss, Faye Wakeling, and Pamela Brown search the Scriptures to document their vision of the church.

Before we gathered at Cedar Glen, I asked each of the participants to do some private Bible study. I asked them to bring a biblical passage that spoke to them about this transition time in the church—a passage through which God was speaking to them. Each of us shared our passage, and we talked about it a little.

At this point in our journey together, we had a strong need to hear what God might be saying to us.

You'll need a Bible in your hand in order to read this chapter.

Living through the wilderness

Marion Best: I want to talk about Exodus chapter 16. I looked at a number of passages, and really wanted to let this one go. But it called back to me again.

It tells the story of the people out in the wilderness, of the whole congregation of Israelites wandering in the wilderness and complaining to Moses: "...If only we'd died by the hands of the Lord in the land of Egypt... for you have brought us out into this wilderness to kill the whole assembly..." (Exodus 16:3).

I deeply believe that what has been, cannot continue to be the same way again.

The Israelites can't go back to Egypt because God called them **out** of Egypt. What if God is calling us out of **what** we've been and **who** we've been?

God called them out and they were only out there a few weeks when they started complaining. They are just out a short time and already they are anxious. Then God provides for them in this wilderness, but they don't like what God provides. This flaky stuff, this manna, they don't even recognize as food. And then some of them start hoarding and don't trust that there'll be enough for tomorrow.

I find myself caught in that story, wishing things could be the way they were—the way I remember them. I know in my soul that they can't be because globally and culturally, whether you want to call it God's judgment or God's beckoning, things have changed.

What things about your congregation would be hardest to change?

And things have to change even more. There are too many inequities and there's been too much disregard for God's creation for things to continue the way they've been. This momentous change in which the church is simply caught up, is part of that.

But what if it's God's doing? What if it's God calling us out of Egypt? I find that disturbing because I do think we're in a wilderness. When we're in the wilderness it seems as if we go around in circles and there's no way out.

The Israelites were grumbling and complaining and I suspect their leadership didn't always know what to do either. And yet God did provide. Sometimes the way God provides isn't what we're looking for, so maybe we have to be open to surprises and not be too anxious. It's hard not to be anxious.

I suspect the grumblings and the murmurings were based in

In what way is your congregation in the "wilderness?"

What is God providing for us, that we may not be noticing?

Israelites' fear and sense of loss. And that's familiar to us. Maybe we're only at the beginning of what will be a long period in the wilderness for our church.

You don't do **nothing** during that period. But how do we decide what to **do**? It seems to me that one of the things we do is stay in touch with the source of our strength. For the Israelites, that was clearly God. This is a really important thing and so I think prayer and remembering who we are will be essential to our survival.

We didn't just come from nowhere. We have roots. We have ties with these Israelites, and all the others since, who have found themselves wandering in the wilderness. So I have this yearning to stay rooted. But at the same time I have to realize that a lot of what I've called familiar and a lot of what I've counted on may not be what God wants for us right now.

Differing responses

Pamela Brown: I grew up in the Anglican Church. We said the same things and we sang the same things week after week. I can sing the *Magnificat*, the *Nunc Dimittis*, the *Te Deum*, and the *O Be Joyful* without it even going through my brain.

But what I've come back to time and time again is the *Magnificat*, because this reflects my experience of working with women.

And I chose to bring the King James Bible because this is the version that I learned and that we sang it in.

Luke 1:46–56: My soul doth magnify the Lord, and my spirit hath rejoiced in God my Savior. For he hath regarded the

Does the Magnificat reflect your experience of God?

low estate of his handmaiden... he hath scattered the proud in the imagination of their hearts. He hath put down down the mighty... and exalted them of low degree.

In the course of preparing to be here I spoke with two women who show me the two poles that I suppose we might find in any congregation.

One of these women has a sense of celebration. She's been in the United Church for 40 years, coming in through the UCW. She would say, "the UCW has been my life, my love, my community, my experience of God."

Just 2 months ago her husband died very suddenly. Her salvation has been her UCW community. She still goes out to all the meetings, all the Presbyterials, all the committees, all that she has always done. And the *Magnificat* has been for her something about the mercy and the care of God in her worst time.

The other woman is about 50. She recently left a 27 year marriage. She had grown up in the church with her whole family fully involved, including herself. Her Dad was on the board, her Mom was in the UCW. They would be regarded as good United Church people.

Her husband did not support the church so there was a lot of anger and resentment and battling over whether the children needed to go or not.

Three years ago she left that marriage, having entered a time of crisis of remembering incest in her home. She realized she had constructed her view of God and of church very carefully and thought she had it well contained in a box. She could open the lid and pull out just the pieces that she needed.

When she remembered the incest experience and realized that this had taken place in a "good church family" everything blew apart for her. She didn't find support in her congregation. Her minister virtually ignored her very clear pleas for help. He asked her, in the middle of a very large group, "Oh, and how are things going after all your troubles?"

But she kept coming back to the *Magnificat* from which she could begin to build a sense of her own spirituality, a sense that maybe there was something somewhere in the church for her.

Fortunately she decided to take a couple of Bible courses at the Atlantic School of Theology, and ran into some excellent scholarship, very supportive theology, and is beginning to rebuild. In that setting she was permitted—no, required—to question, to reflect, to express doubts. These were novel, exciting experiences for her. But she'll not be back in the United Church for a while until she has some sense that she'll find, there, something of the hope and the vision that is in this passage.

With which of these two people would you most identify?

So holding those two in contrast and hearing them both speak

*What does
Mary's song
in the Bible
say to your
congrega-
tion?*

of this passage, is a very powerful thing for me. I see those two extremes. One woman says the church doesn't need to change anything. "It's been wonderful for me. We just have to find a way to get the young women into the UCW." And the other says, "For me it all fell apart and I'm only just beginning to rebuild it. I feel deeply connected to my friends and supporters spiritually, but I don't know about the institutional church."

The gift of faith
Roland Kawano: I have two passages. The first one has haunted me for many years.

John 10:7–18: "I am the good shepherd...Other sheep I have that do not belong to this fold; I must bring them also, and they will listen to my voice. So there will be one flock, one shepherd."

*What has
been your
experience
with people
of other faith
groups?*

When my grandmother died, she died a Buddhist. But my mother, who spent some time with her before she died, remembered that Grandma talked about Jesus—felt good about Jesus.

Several years ago in Los Angeles I found a museum the Japanese Americans have developed because of their wartime experiences. It's in an old Buddhist temple. They have a database of the war relocation records of all the Japanese Americans who were taken off to concentration camps. I'm able to track down this particular grandma and some other relatives. It gives basic information—name, date, education and religion. This grandma puts down "Christian." That just blows my mind.

Then there's a funny kind of parable that's haunting me.

Matthew 13:24–30: "When the plants appeared and grew grain, then the weeds appeared as well... [The farmer] said, 'In gathering the weeds you would uproot the wheat as well. Let both of them grow together until the harvest.'"

There's a new sense of what food and grain and growth is. What we've done with wheat and with our grain genetics is to develop monocultures around the world. If the monoculture fails then these whole economies fail because what they are based on is too narrow—too selective.

Genetic technology today makes us very vulnerable. What would "tares" be? They might have some absolutely essential genes in them. So perhaps we need to let them grow.

I'm thinking of our sense of identity and what we want to be in the United Church. What are the new genes in our United Church genetic pool?

I wonder if this parable is a way of saying to us that we shouldn't be making some judgments now. Judgment comes only at the end. We won't know what wheat and tares are till we see what this genetic pool is like and then we can make some decisions.

Do we have subtle ways of keeping the new "genes," the new ideas, out of our church life?

Strangers and aliens

Phyllis Airhart: I picked some verses from Ephesians. I chose this because I think it offers a very different picture from the church as we usually experience it. It's a very powerful image to me of the type of community that we're called to create—a community that transcends our particular differences.

Ephesians 2:17–22: "You are no longer strangers and aliens, but you are citizens with the saints in the household of God... with Jesus Christ himself as the cornerstone. In him the whole structure is joined together and grows into a holy temple..."

Most of us on our journeys experience that sense of moving towards a household. We're going towards a city. Going home. But we are with other strangers. I think part of our call as Christians is to transcend that experience of alienation from other people.

In my work as a teacher at the Toronto School of Theology

about half the people I deal with are from outside the United Church tradition. And so that verse speaks very powerfully of moving together and becoming less alienated, becoming less like strangers as we build the dwelling place for God.

Who in your church, is a "stranger" to you? What should you do about this?

But we can experience just as much alienation and distance of being a stranger with people in our own church community. The people in our own denomination are often strangers to us.

I feel as if I am part of a movement that is rooted in Christ as the cornerstone. Yet we have a good deal of freedom to work out the particular way we choose to travel. So I have a sense of proceeding with confidence because we are well rooted.

Voices of poverty

Faye Wakeling: I've chosen a passage that I hope in some way will bring the voices of those who live in poverty to our midst. They're women who have, unfortunately, a long experience of poverty. And they continually crack open passages of the Bible for me and I see them through a whole different perspective. So I offer this rather strange passage because for me it says something to us about our future.

The parable of the gold coins; one that we often read in our church. We usually think it's about how we use our talents and our gifts.

Luke 19:11–27: "Then [the trader] said to the bystanders, 'Take the money from him and give it to the one who has ten... To those who have, more will be given; but from those who have nothing, even that will be taken away.'"

Do you have a personal experience of poverty? Do you have any really poor people in your church?

The women in my group at St. Columba were furious when we read this passage. They said, "Boy! Things don't change. That sounds like just now. They elect whoever they want. They elect evil people who have nothing to do with what our lives are about. They continue to do things that benefit them, everything that happens continues to feed those who are rich. Those who are poor continue to get nothing."

These women in poverty who read this passage with me felt that the King was demanding that people cooperate in the system. The person who was called a "good servant" was the one who cooperated—who got more money for an evil king through a corrupt system. Then he was put in charge of more cities and got more power. Those who cooperate in this capitalist society that's destroying all of us at the bottom are rewarded every time.

So we talked for a long time about this, and finally asked, "Okay. Then why is a story like that in the Bible?"

Well, we looked at what came before this passage and what came after. One of the women looked back at the Zacchaeus story just before that, and noticed that it ends with Zacchaeus giving to the poor. And Jesus says at the very beginning of this parable that the disciples supposed the kingdom was to come immediately.

So the women felt that this passage was a reality test. This is what the world is like. This is what they're up against. We hear about Zacchaeus giving to the poor but the system is moving even more to evil and corruption and power.

This was a warning that it was a long, tough job ahead. Jesus saw this on his way to Jerusalem.

This passage was important for this gathering of women in poverty because it raises the questions from a totally different perspective. Some people cannot read this as a liberating passage. In fact it's not about sharing talents—it's about sharing our privilege. And I think that's a real challenge for us in the United Church at this time—to share our privilege and our resources.

My frustration is that I am sharing their words and that's not sufficient. I wish you could hear the voices of people who read this gospel out of their very different experience. Without that we'll continue to serve our own ends. Not out of any ill will, but because we don't see their experience and we don't understand.

Are you willing to share your privilege? What are some of them? How can you share them?

Politics
Alan Barss: I couldn't pick one passage so I picked three. They're all from the New Testament and that may in itself say something about my experience in the United Church.

Luke 17:20–21: "The kingdom of God is not coming with things that can be observed; nor will they say, 'Look, here it is!' or 'There it is!' For, in fact, the kingdom of God is among you."

Some Pharisees had asked Jesus when the kingdom of God would come. His answer was the kingdom of God does not come in such a way as to be seen. No one will say, "Look here it is!" Or, "There it is!" Because the kingdom of God is within you.

The second passage I chose represents to me the political

aspect of the church—the way the church can, when it chooses, respond to injustices that it sees in society. And it's the Jesus-teacher-mad-and-wild passage. It describes the anger that Jesus felt.

John 2:13–17: "In the temple he found people selling cattle, sheep, and doves, and the money- changers seated at their tables. Making a whip of cords, he drove them all out of the temple... He told those who were selling... 'Stop making my Father's house a marketplace...'"

And the third passage I chose is from the second chapter of James and it simply builds on that second passage of faith and how it is really meaningless without some action.

Are you able to put your faith to work in your Monday-Saturday life?

James 2:14–17: "What good is it... if you say you have faith but do not have works... Faith by itself, if it has no works, is dead."

I guess that's why I moved into politics, because it seems to me that there I can put my faith to work.

God's forgotten language
Jim Sinclair: I picked the story of Jesus and the woman with the flow of blood that Luke combines with the story of Jairus and his daughter.

Luke 8:40–56: "She came up behind him and touched the fringe of his clothes... Then Jesus asked, 'Who touched me?'... When the woman saw that she could not remain hidden, she came trembling, and fell down before him... He said to her, 'Daughter, your faith has made you well. Go in peace.'"

Dreams are called "God's forgotten language." And this passage has some of the qualities of a dream. I see parts of myself in it. If I look at this passage as if it was one of my own dreams, I'd see myself in various roles in the dream. And I'm just thinking, if I was the church as I see the church now, what would it mean for Christ to come to me?

In this story, the crowd around Jesus is not unlike the church. It's a group of people who have a mission. They're heading somewhere to something they see as an emergency. And it's almost as if they're carrying Christ along with them as opposed to Christ leading them.

Is Christ leading our congregation or are we leading Christ?

Then within the crowd there is this person who represents that part of me that's been marginalized, dissipated and exploited. And as that hurting person, I am feeling power by being part of the crowd and touching Christ's garment. But I'm still just part of the crowd. And then the real healing occurs when Christ turns to me and brings me back into the community. And then I'm healed, but not just healed and pushed off to the side again, but I'm really embraced by the circle.

Then the dream goes on and I see myself as the dead child, or those around me think I am dead. I feel that. And Christ's attitude is, no you are not dead. But the people around me weep for that part of me that's died. I weep for it.

But that part of me is called back to life. And so I, as the church or part of the church, am often off on my own agenda when the real work is that which Christ points us to.

We are content to leave people by the side and let them catch up with us no matter how long they've been marginalized or regardless of why they're marginalized. They've got to come on our terms. And the story tells me about the nature of Christ who invites us, but never requires us, to come. It's an invitation. "Your faith has made you well."

How can your faith help make the church well?

But then another part of this dream-story is the way it represents my yearning for the church. I don't believe we are dead as a church. I believe that people may see us as dead. They may see us as dead because they define life in a way that is different from the way life should be.

If we're faithful as a church then we'll recognize the times that Christ has called us to get up, find some nourishment and to be active.

From death to life

Marion Pardy: I'd like to take us back to the story of the Hebrew exodus.

Numbers 21:4–9: "The people spoke against God and against Moses, 'Why have you brought us out of Egypt to die...?' Then the Lord sent poisonous serpents among the people... And the people came to Moses and said, 'We have sinned by speaking against the Lord and against you...' So Moses made a serpent of bronze and put it on a pole; and whenever a serpent bit someone, that person would look at the serpent of bronze and live."

Has this ever happened to you in your life—that the cause of death became the symbol of life? In your congregation?

I read this story and at first I said, "Awful!" Then I ended up getting really excited about it.

I thought the story was awful because, as bad as they were with all that grumbling and complaining, God decides to send a bunch of snakes to kill the people. Then the people confess and plead with Moses. Moses prays to God and they have a bronze serpent that becomes the symbol of life. That's what I found exciting. The cause of death becomes the symbol of life! Like the cross!

Then I returned to Exodus 19 and 20 which is the story of the giving of the Ten Commandments. Because it seems to me the commandments came out of the question, "How do we live together in a community?"

I picked that up because I think the call for us now in the church is to stand again at Mount Sinai. We've got to stand again at the cross. We've got to stand again at every pivotal spot along the journey. We need to look at new paradigms, new concepts, new symbols and develop some basic core convictions about that.

How we behave in church and everywhere is greatly influenced by our stories and symbols. Those stories and symbols need to be retold and recreated and reborn in order for something new and transforming and more faithful to the gospel to emerge.

Called to rejoice
Ed Searcy: Lots of times I've really been able to relate to the story of the exodus or of being exiles living in a foreign land. That felt appropriate. But that sets the church up as being right about everything, as having all the truth. Everything else is Babylon—as if ours is the pure community trying to keep alive the faith.

So this passage is about restoration of the community of faith—of the church itself.

Nehemiah 8:1–3, 8–12: "All the people gathered together in the square... And they told the scribe Ezra to bring the book of the law of Moses... So they read from the book of the law of God, with interpretation. They gave the sense, so that the people understood... And the people went their way... rejoicing because they had understood..."

We're on very strange turf. The assembly we're talking about is already here. We're settled in and we're doing well. We live in a very prosperous community. This story of restoration is about a community that needs to do some remembering. Because they were warned, "Be careful when you prosper in the promised land so that you don't forget." This is a message to a community that has forgotten, a community that is seeking to recover its identity.

This is a culture with amnesia. And in order to be alive in a world of many different cultures it needs its memory. So this is the story of the scribe standing up in the square and reading the book of the law of Moses. These are not the regulations they are read-

How much of our identity as a congregation is tied up with our history—our past?

ing. These are the stories about Adam and Eve and Cain and Abel and Joseph and Sarah and Abraham and Miriam and Moses. They read the whole story. They read this and everybody, all the people, men and women and all those who could understand listen. And after they hear it they weep. They wept to hear their story again.

But Nehemiah and Ezra said, "Don't weep! Go and eat and drink and send portions to those for whom nothing is there." So the community is being regathered. Part of that means to celebrate being community and to make sure the poor are fed. That's what you do when you read this story again. You're reminded of who you are. "Do not be grieved, the joy of the Lord is your strength."

The next day they gather and they have a ritual that's interesting. They create booths. It is sometimes called the "ritual of the homeless people." In other words, you who live in big fancy houses go and live as a homeless person for the next week. Remember what it's like to be homeless wanderers and to trust in the Lord. This is where your memory will be strong. The feast of tabernacles.

Are you ashamed of your Christian heritage? How often do you refer to it in conversation? Are there things about your heritage that you should reject even though you feel sentimental about them?

The story speaks of the formation of a unique, strange, peculiar and odd people in the world. A people who are being called to rediscover what it means to be Christians—whether that's United Church or not, I'm not sure—without being ashamed to be distinctively Christian, and without being arrogant about it.

People in other faith groups, other people of goodwill—they need us to be **us**. It doesn't help the Buddhists in our dialogue, if we can't tell them what it means to be Christian. We have a lot of amnesia to get over—a collective memory to recover.

Sharing brokenness
Mardi Tindal: The road to Emmaus is what called to me. In my own experience it's been in those moments of sitting around tables breaking bread that broken hearts are shared; where for a moment

we say, "Yes, that was the Christ. That's what the story was about." It's in those moments of sharing brokenheartedness that we are able to take heart and see Christ.

Luke 24:13–35: "Two of them were going to a village called Emmaus... While they were talking and discussing, Jesus himself came near... but their eyes were kept from recognizing him... When he was at table with them, he took bread, blessed and broke it, and gave it to them. Then their eyes were opened, and they recognized him... The same hour, they got up and returned to Jerusalem... and they told... how he had been made known to them in the breaking of the bread.

Sometimes we don't recognize what's happening to us as we walk along the road. We don't recognize the Christ. But there are moments when we go, "Aha! Yes, now it all falls into place. That's what the story's about."

Do you know what your story is about? When did that discovery happen for you?

Sometimes at camp the staff say to me, "This is one of the only safe places in my life." They're not just talking about their homes, they're talking about their schools and the violence they have to live with. It's sharing brokenheartedness. "Yes! Christ **is** in our midst."

Sometimes my kids aged 12 and nine will get all excited about chaos theory. They just read *Jurassic Park* and they're talking about fractiles and chaos theory and I want to be able to say, "Yeah, yeah! It's continuous you see! **Our** story connects with this." And it does, somehow, but part of our challenge as a church is to figure out exactly how.

When I tell my story of brokenheartedness you don't feel **my** pain. But what I enable you to do is to feel your **own** brokenheartedness. Then together, we are able to take heart. It is in those moments that we are able to see Christ breaking bread in our midst. And seeing that, the story makes sense. There is continuity.

We still have to know the story—you have to be reminded of

When others tell their stories of broken-heartedness, have you really listened? Do we, as a church community, really listen?

the story—and that whole concern about the transmission of values that Faye spoke of.

Often the values we transmit are only cerebral or social. It seems to me values also have to be transmitted in a spiritual way and in a faith community to really take hold. So it's bringing the story into connection with our experience of meeting the Christ.

For group discussion:

Here are suggested discussion topics related to each of the passages used above. (There are also some general discussion questions on the next page.) Pick and choose to suit your own congregation. To help with your understanding, please use a modern translation of the Bible when working with these passages.

Marion Best: Exodus 16—Is God calling our congregation out of what we have been and who we have been, into something new? In what ways are we denying God, avoiding God, or escaping from God?

Pamela Brown: Luke 1:46–56—How has my church responded to Mary's awareness of God's presence? Who are the "mighty" that will be toppled from their thrones?

Roland Kawano: John 10:7–18—How do people in our congregation think of folk from other denominations? From other faith groups? What needs changing? Matthew 13:24–30—What does this parable say to our congregation? What or who are the "tares" or weeds?

Phyllis Airhart: Ephesians 2:17–22—What have we done to increase the sense of alienation from other congregations? From other denominations? From other faith groups?

Faye Wakeling: Luke 19:11–27—There are two ways to read this parable, as Faye has indicated. Are there people in our congregation or in our community who read it the way Faye's friends read it? How do you read it?

Alan Barss: Luke 17:20–21, John 2:13–17, James 2:14–17—Do these passage express what our congregation is about? Which of these would you select to put on a large banner for the front of your church?

Jim Sinclair: Luke 8:40–56—Is our congregation so caught up in all its activities that Christ's presence is ignored? Do we hear the invitation? Where do we find the nourishment so we can live?

Marion Pardy: Numbers 21:4–9—What stories and symbols are most important to us in our congregation? What are the symbols of death? Of life? Where are these stories leading us?

Ed Searcy: Nehemiah 8:1–3, 8–12—The people of Nehemiah's time rediscovered the Word. What would it mean for our congregation to rediscover the Word? Would we weep? Rejoice? What would we do?

Mardi Tindal: Luke 24:13–35—When we gather as a church community, how is "Christ made known" to us? To any visitors who might be with us? How is "Christ made known" to the people in the city or town where we live?

Some general discussion questions:
Where is God calling our congregation? What can I personally do to help this happen?

What are the spiritual needs of our congregation? What are my personal spiritual needs? What can we do to meet those needs?

CHAPTER 6

Into the future

It's always tempting, at events like this, to try to come up with an "answer" or a "solution." Well, it would be silly, if not arrogant, for us to determine what you should be doing in your congregation. And, in fact, you may find, as you work through these discussions, that what you have are simply better, more sharply focused questions. Those are often more useful than overly simple solutions that don't generally work.

As we came to the end of our time at Cedar Glen, we felt the need to bring things to some kind of useful conclusion. We had looked at our past, at our context, at the problems in our congregations, at our leadership, at our biblical roots.

But now we need to move forward. Maybe it would help to begin by asking why we stay in the United Church.

Marion Best sums up the consensus of the group: "There are no quick and easy solutions!"

Where would I go?

*Why do you
stay in your
congrega-
tion? In the
United
Church?*

Phyllis Airhart: Why do I stay in the church? Well, I wonder, is there another church where I would rather be? It's not a perfect church. But where would I find a perfect church?

Faye Wakeling: My struggle with the United Church has always been very much back and forth. The United Church has been the place where I have been continually challenged. I have been allowed to participate at various levels in the church and have had an incredible chance to be involved in groups that looked at different questions and struggled with them.

I live in Montreal which is so multicultural, multilingual, where everything is questioned. It's a very, very different kind of community to be in.

I feel the challenge to make the church keep up with where other people are going, where popular movements are going, where women's groups are going, where solidarity groups involving union people and all kinds of other groups are going. We're looking at incredible problems around this world.

The United Church is not leading any more and I'm trying to come to terms with what that means. Our United Church ethos seems to be so middle-class! I have some real sorrow that we don't find ways to be open to the wonderful learnings and leadings and pushings that are outside beyond us.

And yet I'm hanging in with the United Church because this church has a tremendous capacity to raise questions, to challenge structures and systems. It has had the courage to do this throughout its history. The contextual nature of our church, rooted in what our experience as Canadians in this country has been, and continues to be, is very important. The incredible commitment to con-

Christian Canada

The Religion Poll [by the Angus Reid Group] portrays Canada as an overwhelmingly Christian nation, not only in name but in belief. The poll illustrates that Christianity in Canada has undergone a profound metamorphosis outside—and sometimes alienated from—the mainstream churches. Fewer than a quarter of Canadian adults attend religious services weekly—another eight percent go at least once a month. But eight out of 10 Canadians affirm their belief in God, and two thirds of all adults subscribe to the basic tenet of Christianity—the death and resurrection of Jesus. Almost a third of the adult population claims to pray daily and more than half to read the Bible or other religious literature at least occasionally. "What we've caught here," says [Queens University historian] George Rawlyk, "is Canadian religion changing fundamentally before our eyes."
Maclean's, April 12, 1993

*Is your con-
gregation
keeping up?
Should it be?*

necting that in a global way has been very important.

So I don't see another alternative. But we have not revisioned our role in this society. This society has changed drastically from when I grew up in this church. Everything around us has changed, and there's a real sadness as I watch us fail to come to terms with that. My three children and my two stepchildren have no place in our church even though they're wonderful kids with a real sense of faith as they try to work out the challenges that face them. But the church is not speaking to them. For me it's not the question of how we get them into the church, but how is the church going to get out there and be where people are moving and asking questions.

Do you want your congregation to be an agent for social change? Or an island of stability?

Alan Barss: I really feel a need to keep in touch with God. That aspect of my life is a very important part of who I am. It's something I need to keep working on and keep developing because that's what shapes my actions, who I am and what I do and how I do it.

The **people** in the United Church keep me in it. I've been involved in several congregations and always there have been people who have been willing to struggle—willing to talk about their faith in a very open way.

I talk to a lot of people who are very frustrated with the structures of the United Church and how bureaucratic it is. There are all sorts of documents and task forces and things dealing with the structure of the church. But at the same time I can't think of any church that is more democratic. It allows people to express their opinions at every level, be it local, regional or national. I think that's very important.

What keeps you in your congregation: the people, the organization, or your own history of belonging...?

It allows for tremendous diversity, but it allows for that diversity to be expressed. It's painful and it's awkward and it's clumsy but at the same time it is very valuable.

I sometimes ask people, "Why are you in the United Church?" Many of them say it's because this church has courage to deal with things. This church is a safe place for us to be because it's open and inclusive.

Taking care of my path
Mardi Tindal: For me the real question is, Why would I leave? This is my home. I'm walking the path that I've inherited and feel called to care for it.

A couple of years ago I asked Jim and Alf Dumont if they'd let me produce a video with them in dialogue. They're two brothers who share an Anishinabe mother, a French Canadian father, a United Church upbringing and graduation from Emmanuel College, which is a theological school. But they don't share the same spiritual path.

Following graduation from Emmanuel, Jim knew that he had another path to follow and he set about the hard work of discovering what his traditional native roots were. He now teaches traditional native spirituality at Laurentian University.

Alf went on to be ordained in the United Church and was the first Speaker of the All-Native Circle Conference. It occurs to me now that even producing such a video is a distinctly United Church thing to do.

In the midst of the taping Jim spoke most compellingly about how the Creator gives us different paths to walk. And we have to be careful to know and understand the path that the Creator's given us. We have to take care of that path. And then we can build bridges of respect with people who are walking other paths.

My main temptation is to make an idol of the United Church. I have to face this potential sin. But I think the United Church ethos is something God enjoys. And it's something I have to walk with and take care of.

I guess we all have to come to terms with our roots in one way or another. I went back for my third summer of directing a United Church camp, after a 17 year absence. There was an 18-year-old last summer whose grandfather was a United Church minister. Like you, Ed, his parents met smoking behind a tree at that United Church camp. Now they're not involved in the church, though they're very active in their communities.

I asked this teenager to read *Living God's Way*, Ralph Milton's book of biblical stories. He came to me and said, "This is such a great book! This isn't how I remember the Bible. And this is great stuff." He had been taught more about traditional native spirituality than about Christianity and he was delighted to discover that Christianity also offered spiritual insights.

Others said to me, "Thank you for morning watch—the morning worship service." I thought they'd think it was too religious. But at the end of the summer they said the worship was one of the highlights. They said their only option in high school and on campus was to be part of a Christian community that they

What "path" is God calling you personally to walk? What about your congregation?

Feeding the spirit as well as the mind, the group takes time for a hymn from _Songs for a Gospel People._

describe as "fascist." It's a group that they feel is very intolerant toward many people including those who are gay and lesbian. They are sure that intolerance would never happen in the United Church community. That's why they identify themselves with the United Church. That's one of the reasons I think our ministry is so important to them.

Could that "fascist" attitude happen in your congregation?

The point is that we must not allow our path of faithfulness to grow over and disappear. Others often need and want to hear the wisdom from our tradition and story.

But mostly, this is the community where I've been warmly loved and where I've learned to love beyond the ethnic community called the United Church.

It must have been quite a thing for my grandparents to move from being Methodists to United Church. Maybe they had second thoughts by the time they came to the end of their lives. But the differences between me and my grandchildren will be even greater than between me and my grandparents. So I have to be prepared for at least that much change.

Ed Searcy: Why do I stay in the United Church? Because I'm halfway to the pension fund, I suppose!

My life is so caught up in the church that even if I wanted to leave, it's very difficult to imagine how I would, with five dependents and a big mortgage. I would still be United Church even if I wasn't a minister though.

Have you had any "mentors" in the United Church? Who?

In the United Church I have a group of colleagues whom I really like and would like to be with more—men and women of different ages I respect very much and whose company I enjoy. We were talking last night about Ralph Donnelly dying. Ralph was a mentor of mine. He had an ability to laugh and scream about the church and yet take it very seriously. That has profoundly affected me.

I find congregations very difficult to understand and live with. And yet I really find myself falling in love with the people—with their faithfulness and their giftedness.

My vision of the Church that's birthing is of a congregation of people who are caught up by the dream of what community could be.

Last year a woman with a long story of abuse came and said, "I've got a problem. I have reason to believe my ex-husband is going to come and try to get my daughter when I'm in church." We realized we had to make our church a safe place for her. It was very difficult to do, and it was painful. But we grew in the process. And the woman felt very affirmed and included by the process, even though she was afraid she might be ostracized. And it brought out a number of stories from other people who had experienced similar pain. This was not a fake place of smiling people but people who recognized that something important was happening.

For those reasons I put up with going to Conference Executive meetings and living through long frustrating council meetings and feeling overwhelmed by too many people and being too busy.

The boomers have it

High rates of interfaith marriage and continuing large numbers of blended families will result in new generations of children with weak institutional religious ties. Denominational boundaries within Protestantism will likely erode further as increasing numbers...grow up knowing very little about their religious heritages. Better known will be the general faith traditions—Roman Catholicism, Judaism, Islam and Protestantism clustered into its liberal and conservative camps. A highly privatized and relativistic approach to religion, already practiced by large numbers of boomers, will probably become even more widespread in a society that has no strong religious center."

Wade Clark Roof
A Generation of Seekers,
Harper San Francisco, 1993, p. 249

How would you, in your congregation, have responded to this situation?

The best part of Canada

Marion Pardy: I think we are at a crisis in the church—we're in transition—and that feels a little scary. I'm not sure that we as a church are going to make the most helpful decisions. Part of that may be where I'm presently working and living in Newfoundland. The old evangelical in me thinks that the good news Jesus talked about is focused on the world and because of that, we have something to say to the world through the institutionalized church.

Is there a crisis in your congregation? Your community? Your region?

Pamela Brown: I think the privilege of being a lay person within the United Church is wonderful. I don't feel the kind of vulnerability and risk that I hear coming from some of the clergy. The times of connection and reflection and stretching and clarification and struggling and coming through the other side, have been just wonderful.

Do you enjoy struggling with questions? Or do you want someone to tell you the answers?

It is getting harder to maintain that kind of momentum in the Church. But I find I have just as many questions as I did 20 years ago and just as few answers. But there's no way I'm going to quit on any of it because it's life-giving for me. That's why I'm in it still and will remain. The United Church was the best thing about emigrating to Canada.

Marion Best: Why do I stay here? Where else would I go? The church has been my mentor. It's been home. Through my involvement with the church I've come up against people who were different from me culturally, economically, philosophically and in terms of the spectrum of faith. That's been really rich.

1988 and the gay ordination issue for me was a time of feeling hopeful and then struggling to keep that hope alive. I felt somehow we were going to fragment—the United Church was just going to come apart. I suppose 1988 was a very important watershed in the life of the church. For the first time we

Discerning the Spirit

Since the late 1960s, congregations of the United Church of Canada have tended to assume that ... "discerning between spirits" can be experienced through layers of accountable government, due process, parliamentary procedure, and the eventual consensus of the people. Trust, personal initiative, spontaneity, and the in-breaking of God are verbally praised, but structurally discouraged, in an effort to enforce whatever is "politically correct" or "loyal to our heritage."

Again, the public are not stupid. They perceive that the expectation that a congregation can be gripped by a vision of church transformation, **through consensus,** is like expecting an alcoholic to be gripped by a vision of health through consultations with his drinking buddies at the local bar. It's possible, but unlikely.

Thomas G. Bandy
from "Discerning between spirits"
in *PMC: the Practice of Ministry in Canada,*
September 1994

Do you ache over these hurtful things we do to each other? Are there others in your congregation who are also aching?

faced the possibility of fragmentation in a way that I had not seen before. So that's still a concern for me.

I ache at the hurtful things we do to one another. It's not that I have an answer. It's just that I ache and I know others do too.

Jim Sinclair: Why am I here? The Church exhausts me and it excites me.

The things that excite me, for the most part, are the people in my congregation. That's what sustains me from week to week.

Has your church given you strength to deal with difficult things?

I don't regard myself as a very brave person but I've found myself in situations where I've done things or said things that I know I would never have done if I didn't have other strong people in the denomination standing with me.

That's what I mean about it exhausting me sometimes. I hear people saying, "Why can't we just relax for a while? Why must we always be on to new issues?" Yet that is one thing that energizes me. There is a struggle for momentum and it rests sometimes inordinately in some places more than others.

What would you miss if your congregation disappeared?

I think I'd miss too much if I wasn't in the United Church. I can't find another church that quite does it for me in the way that the United Church does, because justice and hope are motifs that are in my bones.

We're just too busy

Marion Best: It's helpful to focus on the things that keep us in the United Church, on the values that we celebrate there. Because then we know what it is that we want to protect. We know what is important. But let's focus for awhile on some of the practical problems that we face in being United Church congregations.

Pamela Brown: We're having a lot of trouble getting a new chair for the nominating committee. The present chair, who's done the job four years, says he's absolutely worn out. There just aren't enough people to do all the jobs. So what's going wrong? People don't want to do those jobs in the church any more.

Why don't people want to do those jobs any more?

Ed Searcy: Almost any church person could tell a similar story, Pam. We're so busy just trying to keep being what we are, it's hard to imagine how we're going to ever do anything new. If I put a note in the bulletin saying we're going to have a meeting on

Tuesday night to talk about the future of the church, I wonder if anyone will come.

Marion Best: In all my years of activity in the United Church, I know that some of those things have been "spirit filled" and some have been "soul destroying." It seems to me the things that were spirit filled were when my gifts were used. They were soul destroying when I tried to keep something going that I didn't really believe in.

If you're having trouble getting anybody to do those things, you might ask if the thing is worth doing.

Phyllis Airhart: Is there any way of restructuring or rescheduling so that you have less frequent meetings or different types of meetings. There are whole groups of people who are automatically eliminated simply by the choice of time the particular group chooses to meet.

Ed Searcy: How do we get off the treadmill? We're caught in a kind of low level depression. And I don't know how to get people to come together and talk about that basic funk.

Pamela Brown: We have trouble even getting people together to engage in this sort of a process.

Do we really care about the future of our church? Or are we just too busy to even think about it?

What things in our congregational life are not really all that important?

Phyllis Airhart emphasizes a point to Marion Best.

Why not? Sunday morning is the only time when we're all together. Well, most of us.

Phyllis Airhart: Would it be a terrible thing if you took a Sunday morning service to do that?

Pamela Brown: I think it would be quite fine.

The gift of Jubilee

Marion Best: We probably need to be a bit careful here. Sometimes there's a feeling in the congregation that the reason for the deep funk is the lackluster performance of the minister. This may or may not be true, but if that perception is there, it needs to be dealt with. So if you feel that way, the first thing to do is talk with your own congregational Ministry and Personnel Committee.

In one instance I know of, the people in the congregation talked to that committee, but didn't feel as if they were getting any action there. So they sent a letter to the Presbytery, because the Presbytery is like the Bishop in some other denominations. It's the Presbytery that is supposed to have oversight of the congregation.

Anyway, in this congregation, a staff person from the Presbytery and a couple of Presbytery volunteers went to visit the congregation. For six months now they have been working with the M&P committee and the minister to try to assess the situation and to suggest things that both the M&P committee and the minister might do. They have kept the people who contacted the

---

Community and belonging

We can glimpse a resolution to these complex questions when we realize that effective churches strive for a healthy balance in the meeting of these various needs: between serving the desires of those already involved in the church and responding to the needs of those beyond the touch of the church, for example.

Identifying committed Christians as consumers also raises questions about the nature of the Christian community. Where is the balance between the needs of the individual consumer and the need for a cohesive Christian community? Individualism suggests that personal needs override collective needs. We live in an increasingly fragmented society and yet the Christian life is built on a model of a shared life with fellow believers.

One of the key "needs" expressed by committed Christians in our survey involves the need for community and belonging. Thus, an important part of what the committed Christian consumer seeks involves characteristics which inherently limit the consumer model. In essence, part of the committed Christian's set of needs involves the sense of belonging to a faith community and the sense of unswerving commitment to biblical standards. Rather than shopping for fragments, these Christians want a meaningful, integrated experience of faith.

by Donald C. Posterski and Irwin Barker, from *Where's a Good Church?* Wood Lake Books, 1993

Presbytery informed. It'll probably be almost a year-long process before that's fully resolved.

Sometimes it's just a case of general weariness on the part of both the minister and the lay people in the congregation.

Mardi Tindal: Jim, you told me about a congregation blessing someone to take a sabbatical—saying to this person, you take a whole year away from committees and other church work.

I'm wondering if a congregation could allow itself to be blessed with a sabbatical year. Part of our problem is that we can't do this kind of congregational futurizing on top of everything else. Well, maybe the congregation can allow itself to be blessed for a year—to put some things on the shelf while it plans its future.

Phyllis Airhart: A Jubilee year.

Ed Searcy: A sabbath year. A really interesting concept. One whole year of fallow—let as many of the programs as possible simply lie fallow for a year.

Faye Wakeling: Imagine doing that for a whole year!

Phyllis Airhart: We could start with a Jubilee Sunday. Or a Jubilee month.

Marion Best: But I want to focus on clergy leadership a bit. One of the best gifts a congregation can give to a minister is three months off.

I wish all ministers who have been in a charge for five years could have three months off. They might want simply to read or do whatever. The trick is to give this to the ministers without it appearing to be a veiled criticism. The gift of a Jubilee time. "We'll pay your salary and we'll carry the ministry while you're away."

Is the relationship between your minister and congregation as open and healthy as it should be?

Is this really practical? Could your congregation do it? What are the absolute essentials?

Proclaim liberty

And you shall hallow the fiftieth year and you shall proclaim liberty throughout the land to all its inhabitants. It shall be a jubilee for you: you shall return, every one of you, to your property and every one of you to your family. That fiftieth year shall be a jubilee for you: you shall not sow, or reap the aftergrowth, or harvest the unpruned vines. For it is a jubilee; it shall be holy to you; you shall eat only what the field itself produces.

Leviticus 25:10–12
New Revised Standard Version
Copyright © 1989, Division of Christian Education of the National Council of Churches of Christ in the USA.

Has your minister (or ministers) had such a sabbatical?

When I worked at Naramata Centre, it was part of the understanding that at the end of the fifth year you got a four month study leave, which you could add to your vacation and your regular continuing education time.

Many United Church congregations don't realize that they are required to give their minister three weeks of study leave every year, in addition to vacation time. And if the Ministry and Personnel Committee are doing their job, they'll **insist** that the minister take that study time.

Any clergy who think they can't take that are cheating both the congregation and themselves.

Alan: We try to be pro-active in that sense. Early in the year we ask our minister, "What are your plans for your study leave?" Then we challenge them a little bit if they're hesitant.

Marion Best: Plus, it would be great for lay people to start planning how they will be the church without the minister for three months. Then some people would really pay attention to worship planning, and this can be a really good growing time for the church. You'd start to line up possibilities and do some training, and figure out which neighboring clergy could be available for crisis stuff.

Another possibility is the exchange. Sometimes clergy do an exchange with someone from Australia or the US or Great Britain, sometimes someone from another province. Then both the minister and the congregation have some new ideas, some new faces, and often a welcome breath of fresh air.

But it requires some open and trusting communication and some creative thinking. When the congregation is in a funk, there

Disintegrating authority

Clericalism—like sin—is carrying a good thing too far. The clear role and authority given to the ordained leader really did and often still does facilitate the mission of the church. But the development of the clergy into a special class with special privilege and considerable power to govern a large institution [results in the concentration of power in the clergy]. Regardless of the polity of the denomination, it is my impression that clergy have, effectively, a veto on every important issue. It they genuinely believe a course of action is wrong, it will not happen.

But...the all-powerful authority of the clergy as a class, is breaking down. Most church members, even clergy, welcome that fact, but they find the resulting arrangements to be confusing and chaotic.

Loren B. Mead
The Once and Future Church
The Alban Institute, 1991, p.33

Lay people leading worship? Preaching? Could you do that?

is usually something creative that can be done that will benefit everyone.

Gathering in the Temple
Jim Sinclair: What about having a Sunday of questions?

I'm thinking of the story of Hezekiah where the messenger arrives and they're going to be plowed under by the opposing army and he doesn't know what to do so he takes the message and goes into the Temple. (2 Kings 19:8–19)

Maybe we set up a process of getting as many questions as possible and then carrying them into worship. But worship might take a different form that day, where people are assigned to take a particular question and work on it in some way. We'd need to do that so that it doesn't look like administration but that it looks like an act of worship.

Mardi Tindal: Anything like that should be part of the whole church school process. Children, seniors—the whole church should be involved.

Ed Searcy: Some of our congregations are not in enough trouble to do that sort of thing. We're doing reasonably well in our congregation, frankly, so there's the attitude, "If it ain't broke, don't fix it."

Alan Barss: I think we'd have the same problem. Why should we be asking these questions?

Mardi Tindal: Are your teenagers saying that everything is relevant and they're real excited about being part of this church for the next 20 years?

Ed Searcy: I've talked to them some and need to talk to them more...

Pamela Brown: There aren't many teenagers in our church, actually.

Mardi Tindal: Maybe we should point that out to the folks who are saying, "Everything's fine!" We need to face the blunt question: Does our church **have** a future?

Phyllis Airhart: But you don't have to look very far to see churches

What would a Sabbath year do for you? For your clergy?

What questions would you want to ask, to have your congregation think about?

Are teenagers an active part of your church?

*Could you
send a team
of folks
around to
other
churches to
gather ideas?*

that are not healthy. If you're doing well, find out why you are strong and keep doing those things. Are there different strategies that your congregation has been using, different choices it made that enabled it to fare as well as it has? Then you can pass that information on to the rest of us.

Who took our church?

Jim Sinclair: I have a fantasy. Oliver North had the capacity to remove himself electronically from photographs so that he didn't show up in meetings that he wasn't supposed to be at. I understand with some computer technologies, that isn't all that hard to do.

Suppose you took some photos of your church. Then electronically remove it. Then put these pictures all over the place, to see if anybody misses you. Or at a Board meeting simply ask, "Any comments about this picture?"

*What differ-
ence would it
make to your
life if your
church wasn't
there?*

Ed Searcy: What difference would it make if we weren't there? But ask the question with a picture!

Jim Sinclair: I remember Walford United Church in northern Ontario. All 23 people came out to the potluck supper. They filled a whole wall with newsprint and put time lines on it—1900, 1920 and so on. Then as we ate supper, people went up and wrote their memories. Grace Walford could remember the train wreck in 1908 when everybody was mobilized to help.

The history was right there in front of them. Then the next thing was to characterize each era. What name do you put on each stage of our history?

*What could
your congre-
gation learn
from looking
at its past?
Would it help
deal with the
future?*

Then finally we ask, what might we learn from that tradition that will help us into the future?

Ed Searcy: Another question every congregation needs to ask is, "What's happening to the UCW?"

Marion Best: Exactly. We're facing some really practical things. The UCW is very concerned about its future, and it has reason to worry. In the Mission and Service fund the biggest drop in contributions is in givings from the UCW. They give 10 percent of the total income of the Mission and Service fund.

They're also often the only group that does a mission study. And the mission study for this year and next year is "Mission into the 21st Century." So even if you can't get any other group in the church to look at the future, at least you might involve the UCW.

Ed Searcy: To mobilize the whole congregation is the best way, obviously. But if that isn't possible, maybe we look for the smaller pockets where we might find receptive groups. The UCW is one. I suspect our Outreach Committee is another.

Marion Best: The UCW would love the Jubilee year idea. No catering for a year!

Marion Pardy: There is something wrong when someone offers three years of their time as chair of the board and then afterwards they just can't wait for that to end: "Thank God that's over." We need to look at the leadership we have and do some kind of affirmation or support of that.

Do you affirm the leaders in your church? Do you make leadership a happy experience for them?

Jim Sinclair: We've been bringing job sharing into the church. And we discovered the synergy of two people working together. In effect we've got a sub-committee of four or five people that suddenly have brought energy.

There was a little church in Seaway Valley which decided that to find the right person for a particular job, they needed to have a profile of that person. There were a bunch of kids around, so they had the biggest person present lie down on a large piece of paper and they cut out a profile. They put it on the wall. Somebody drew a mustache but another group added a skirt. It was just a fun thing, but they got the whole church animated around finding the right person.

I'd love to put a notice in *The Observer* to say, "Are there Bible study groups across the country who would help us with a problem we're working on? Is there a Bible study group out there that would research for us experiences of our grandmothers and grandfathers in the faith out of the scriptural record who had to address what to do when the community was running out of steam?"

A six-week commitment
Marion Best: There's a model that I have worked with around helping congregations look at themselves. Part of that involves six weeks of study in small groups.

There were some things that were done in the whole congregation like looking at our history and looking at our community. But then there was six weeks of study around, "What does it mean to be in ministry? What does it mean to be in mission? What do we believe about the gospel and what do we believe about church?"

The groups were all lay led and held in people's homes. People were phoned and invited and everybody in the congregation got an invitation. The lay leaders were recruited first. Then they looked at the congregational list, divided up the names and called people they knew. Then decided how they would divide up the folks they didn't know. But everyone got a personal invitation.

The response was really very good. In every case people said that was the high point of this year-long program.

I think the key was lay leadership. Lay people were equipped and they had resources. They had some training. They had ongoing support and everyone had an invitation. Everyone knew it would only be one evening a week for six weeks.

Could your congregation organize such a process? Would you want to help organize it? Or to be a participant?

Some chose to go away and do the study over a full weekend, like a retreat. The study was usually done in the fall between about the middle of October and the beginning of December, or just after Christmas, or during Lent. Those were the times of year that people would commit.

Ed Searcy: So to do this process, we might get some outside help. Or we could just use this book, and work at it together as a group. We'd provide one copy for each person, and then get everyone in the church together for a six-week series of study groups.

Black holes

What are you most anxious about?

Jim Sinclair: Let me ask you this. When you think of your church, where are you most anxious?

Pamela Brown: I'm anxious about our buildings—these great dollar-munching monoliths!

Alan Barss: Black holes!

Pamela Brown: Yeah. They gobble up all that we have. Not just our money but our energy. For what?

For young people, these buildings feel foreign. Sitting in rows and listening to somebody up against the wall there is not their idea of spirituality, I don't think.

If we really *are* concerned about young people, then we need really different kinds of spaces—more flexible, more participatory, to make it more possible to do creative things—music, dance, things like that.

Our spaces seem all wrong and they take so much of what we have.

Jim Sinclair: Two women came to me in the last year and a half, both of them retiring, one because of retrenching in her company.

They said they had some excellent resources and processes to help them figure out their pension plan and how to handle their money. But they came to me and said, "I would like you to help me think about what retirement means to me as a spiritual person."

That got me wondering if, as a church, our task is to help lead people through the spiritual issues of life. We need to work with people who are crossing boundaries. Our churches are crossing boundaries.

Marion Best: About a year ago *Maclean's* ran an article that talked about the spiritual hunger in the world and in Canada particularly. Most Canadians are on spiritual quests. The great ma-

Eight marks of an excellent church

The best-selling book by Thomas Peters and Robert Waterman, *In Search of Excellence* (Harper & Row, 1982), is an example of sociological thinking applied to business. They identify eight marks of the excellent business enterprise. This description also applies to an excellent church. Change a few words from business to church terminology, and the eight principles as they apply to the church can be described as follows:

1. **A Bias for Action.** The church succeeds that is willing to try things, knowing that if something doesn't work it will be changed, and that the congregation may well learn from the process what would be effective.
2. **Keep Close to the Community.** The church succeeds that discovers the real needs of the community and seeks to meet them.
3. **Autonomy and Creativity.** The church succeeds that creates what is needed for the particular group of people whom it serves.
4. **Get It Done through People.** The church succeeds that puts people first in its programs and gives priority to training, motivation, and keeping in touch.
5. **Hands-on, Value Driven.** The church succeeds that has decided what to stand for and thus is not afraid to get involved in real-life situations where its values might be challenged.
6. **Stick to the Knitting.** The church succeeds that does more of what it is best at.
7. **Simple Form, Lean Staff.** The church succeeds that keeps it simple, with just enough people involved to do the job.
8. **Simultaneous Loose-Tight Properties.** The church succeeds that combines the maximum freedom to be creative with a tight communications network that keeps everyone in touch with what others are doing.

Clair Woodbury
from *100 Ways to be the Church*
Wood Lake Books, 1991

How do we lead people through the spiritual issues of life? Do we do this consciously in our church, or does it just happen?

jority of Canadians consider themselves spiritual. But they don't go into any church at all.

What if someone came to you and said, "I'm on a spiritual journey. What would I find if I came to your place? What do you have to offer me?"

Offering friendship

Alan Barss: I think of a couple of friends of mine, who have started coming to our church because they both have a need to nurture their spirituality. They are coming to our church initially because my wife Colleen and I and some other friends are there.

Promises

WARRANTY. Many people are attracted to Christ—it's Christians who give them trouble. If you attend our church, WE PROMISE not to tell you how to dress, feel, think, or vote. We won't discourage your questions or insult your intelligence. WE PROMISE to welcome you in Christ's name, involve you in our community if you like or leave you in peace if you'd prefer. WE PROMISE to smile now and then, experiencing with you the joy of life in Christ. If we break this promise, you are entitled to reclaim your misgivings about "organized religion."

The Kitsilano Christian Community,
Vancouver, Summer 1993, p.47
Used by permission.

Marion Best: So you offered them friendship?

Alan Barss: Friendship. Some sense of community. We have an hour after church just sitting around having coffee. We have a big open room beside the sanctuary and every week the coffee pot is on. And there may be croissants or muffins and so the smells of these warm things coming out of the ovens draw people into the room.

There are some very good classes offered every year. We call them confirmation classes.

Phyllis Airhart: Are they just for people who are preparing for confirmation?

Alan Barss: No. The people who go to these classes may have already been confirmed. And not everyone who goes to those classes is confirmed.

Marion Best: Could I ask any question there, or would I be expected to already know something about Christianity? Would they expect I'd know the Bible?

Alan Barss: No. Not at all.

Ed Searcy: Marion, if somebody should ask why they should come to our church, I'd have to say it's because we are a community of people who believe that in Jesus we've discovered what it means to be human beings. Or rediscovered it. We are rediscovering it together in one another.

We don't have the perfect community. We wish it was perfect. We have arguments with one another. We have lots of questions, but we have a community of people who, one way or another, have been mystified, captivated by that vision in some way.

Would it help if we stopped trying to be "perfect" and simply tried to be loving?

We're proud to belong to a tradition that in fact has discovered Christ speaking through not just the clergy or just the lay leaders, but also through the questions of the children or the new people. We'd like to be open to questions, because we believe that that's where the holy may be speaking to us.

So that's why there's the bread baking and the croissants and the communal life. We wish we were more diverse, so we'd love to have you because you look like a different kind of person. We hope you might catch some of the vision that we have and you might bring something of the vision you have to enrich and challenge us. We have an old tradition that forms us and challenges us and we form and challenge it. We live in tension with it and we are nourished by it.

Tired and dispirited
Pamela Brown: Well, that's not us. We really have our back to the wall.

I think people in my downtown urban congregation are looking to be energized. They want some sense of hope that what the church offers will have meaning for them, will answer some of their questions, and will give them a sense of something more than just the habit of showing up at church on Sunday mornings. They would like to hear the promise of a better life, of better relationships, of a better sense of community, of better paths towards justice and reconciliation.

I think we're foundering. And if you have some good suggestions, I think we're ready to hear it. Because we're all tired and somewhat dispirited.

Mardi Tindal: Jim, maybe the photograph of the missing church you suggested. I wonder about publishing it in a local newspaper, with the question, "What would you miss?" And give a phone number.

Mardi Tindal: What would you miss, Pam?

What would
you miss
most, if your
church
weren't there?

Pamela Brown: Well, 130 men and maybe 10 women would miss their Sunday supper. But most of the work and organization for that Sunday supper actually comes from outside of our congregation. The people in our church neighborhood might not mind if the church disappeared. They aren't too keen on our Sunday suppers—all these scruffy individuals littering up the place every Sunday afternoon!"

Last year we had a two-person ministerial team, including an extraordinarily gifted woman who did an amazing job of getting to know who could do what. And things began to happen for a while. But we couldn't sustain the salary, and the vision of what the team could be did not materialize. Letting go of that vision and that hope was very painful for us.

Do you know
how bad
things are?
What are you
avoiding?

Alan Brown: Maybe we need to begin by letting people know how bad things really are. It's a typical political strategy. Paint the bleakest picture possible and raise the flag of Armageddon. If you want to make any sort of fundamental change, people have to be motivated to do that. So if you really want some changes, the first question is motivation.

Resurrection

A sad Ida Scrivener handed over a $700,000 cheque from the sale of her dying Chalmers United Church to the leaders of a Downtown Eastside church ministry Wednesday.

With bearded men sleeping on the benches and pews of First United Church, Scrivener told a gathering of ministers, church members and mentally disabled people she hoped the seeds sown by the sale of 95-year-old Chalmers United Church would produce good crops.

"There's always death and resurrection," said Rev. Jim Elliot, president of the B.C. Conference of the United Church of Canada and a minister at First United.

"The new life can only come when you give up the old. I'm excited about a congregation that dies gracefully. Many don't. They hang on when they shouldn't."

The last will and testament of

Ed Searcy: In our Presbytery we've closed several churches and others are on half-time that used to be full-time.

Before people are willing to change, they have to be uncomfortable enough to **want** to change, but not so uncomfortable they no longer **can** change. Some of our congregations are no longer able to change. There's too much wrong. The trick is to not let ourselves go that long—to change while we still can. Maybe we can start to identify the things that are not working and name them. If, in our congregation, we still can pretend we're comfortable, then we will have a hard job getting heard.

What's still working well in your congregation?

To die creatively

Marion Best: Maybe, on a Sunday morning, we can tell stories of churches. The ones that "died creatively," the ones who didn't have a choice, and the ones who spotted their problems before they became terminal and were transformed.

Is your church being called to die creatively?

In some cases it was cultural shifts that caused the death of a church. Then the most logical thing to do was to close and use the resources in other ways.

You only change when there are more reasons to change than not to change. If you keep denying long enough you will find that you can't change and it's too late.

Maybe from studying scripture we realize that we aren't okay the way we are. Perhaps we're too individualistic, or we are too private about our faith. When we get to these painful

Chalmers donates $700,000 to First United for its ministry to the disenfranchised and also spreads another $1.6 million to nurture the Vancouver School of Theology, Naramata Centre and church development.

A final statement from the few remaining members at Chalmers who will begin attending other United Churches this summer read:

"We hope that our story will be remembered in their story, and our funds will give energy to their mission. We are passing on not only money, but also memory, vision and challenge to those who follow."

Excerpted from an article by Douglas Todd, *The Vancouver Sun*, March 31, 1994 Used by permission.

How do we keep focused on the essential mission of the church so we don't get distracted by all sorts of unimportant things?

transition points in the life of our community, we must begin telling stories and bearing one another's burdens.

There may be a whole bunch of reasons why, but I believe that we can no longer stay the way that we are.

Jim: When one hurts we all hurt. When one rejoices we all rejoice. But if that isn't happening, what is the data we don't have?

Marion Pardy: Whatever we do within the church has to be linked to a reflection on the scriptures. Where is God in all of this?

Prayer and healing

Mardi Tindal: One of the things that's happened in our congregation has been quite wonderful. It began about nine years ago as a Hamilton Conference project on teaching different spiritual disciplines and practices. And it happened to be hosted at Lowville United Church.

At the end of the project no one wanted to stop. It's continued for eight years and new people keep coming all the time. On the second and fourth Wednesday morning of every month there is a spirituality session.

One week might be on Meister Ekhardt and creation-centered spirituality, and another week might have Morton Paterson on abusiveness in the family and the spiritual resources for dealing with that.

So the Lowville Prayer Center has been born and there's energy there. It has generated the spiritual strength for doing more outreach. Spiritually

It's not complicated

The 21st century is when we will do a lot of reversals in our thinking, and finally discover that lay ministry is about ministry in the world. That spirit is slowly growing. It's a kind of revival time; maybe they come at the end of every century. We will see our paid staff doing administration and leadership development and worship focusing, and lay people will be equipped for ministry in the world; caring, sharing and evangelism.

Congregations that are going to be alive will have to find a way to do evangelism in a way that is comfortable for us as United Church people. There will be a real heightening of spirituality. Instead of deciding on an issue and responding to it—a working-out-of-your-head-ministry, which is ineffective—the pattern will be a small group Bible study, where people pray and share and discover their vocations.

It's not complicated. If there were seven or eight people sitting down praying, reading the Bible, talking—even two or three groups like that—a typical congregation would be transformed. We need to minister and serve out of our hearts.

Rev. Jim Dowden, Grimsby, Ontario,
from *The United Church Observer*
June, 1994. Used by permission.

hungry people come. They want to have training in prayer. They want to have days of silence. Healing services have been very important.

A healing service does not just mean laying on of hands for people with physical illness. And the emphasis is on healing, not necessarily curing. There's an attentiveness to what kind of trauma the person or community is feeling, and what kind of healing is needed.

That's not what everybody should do but that's something that's happened in our community that seems to have been energizing.

Marion Best: There are signs of life and hope. And there are signs of decay and death. Some congregations should make the decision to die so that others might live. And there are other congregations that need to take brave risks in order to be God's faithful community. My dream is that the people in the United Church will remember the rich and precious heritage we have—our heritage from the Bible and our heritage from the history we have here in Canada. We can draw on that heritage and work with God to create a faithful future church.

Do we have the courage to live our way into future—to follow where God calls?

Ed, you brought with you a letter from Keith Howard. I think it's about how hope breaks in unexpectedly.

God sends a spy
Ed Searcy: Keith writes for *The Observer*, so you may recognize his name from that, but most of the time he's the minister at Pilgrim United in Victoria.

It's a small church that was totally disseminated after the controversy of 1988. Everybody left except for two people. Only two. All the rest of the members and the minister left.

So the Presbytery put Keith there. He started out as two-thirds time. Now his wife Gaye also shares the ministry as a Staff Associate, half-time. Today it is a lively, vital church.

Many, maybe most of the people at Pilgrim are new to the United Church. They have hardly any background or memory about what it means to be the church. So it's a really interesting case study in what our churches of the future may look like because they have no tradition, no past they have to live down.

I'd like to read you a part of a letter Keith sent to me, because I think it really says something profound about what it might mean to be a United Church congregation that is faithful to God's future. They're rediscovering what it means to be a church.

Easter went well. Too many people. As the place filled I found myself thinking, "I hope I don't have to visit all these people."

The most moving time for me was during baptism.

For the past year or so this ten-year-old girl, Leah, has been coming to worship by herself.

It's okay with her parents if she comes even though they do not. After all "It's her decision" and they don't want "to lay anything on her." She walks to church faithfully every week. Recently the family has moved a lot but she always manages to find a way here.

About six months ago Leah asked the Stewards if she could have offering envelopes. That surprised us because not all the adults take their stewardship that seriously. We sent a note home making sure her parents knew we weren't trying to con this kid out of her lunch money. They said "Fine," and so for the last few months there's always this envelope bearing Leah's name.

Around the beginning of Lent we put this little note in the bulletin saying if there were any folk interested in transferring membership, joining an inquiry class, or wondering about baptism, talk to me. So Leah comes to me one Sunday before worship and says she'd like to be baptized. Never been. She had thought about it all week, talked to her parents, and she wants it to happen. Her parents don't object but are not pushing her either.

"Major theological problem," I say to myself. I took it to session. We had a good discussion about baptism, its meaning and responsibilities. After about an hour, the session decides we will baptize Leah, but not confirm her. Which is proper. We'll make it clear to her that confirmation comes later. So if it's not a baptism-confirmation, does that make it an infant baptism? "Sort of," says the session.

Leah is ten years old. Her parents won't take the vows on her behalf in this "infant" baptism, but we're clear someone else needs to make the commitment. So the Session says they will assume responsibility for Leah over and above their normal congregational responsibilities.

It sounds sort of right to me. Extraordinary, but probably okay. So we vote to go ahead and especially commit her elder to be on the case.

I tell Leah. She's ecstatic.

Gaye meets with her to talk about baptism, makes sure she knows what's happening and what it means. I suspect, in her soul, Leah probably knows better than any of us.

I meet with her and her parents and we talk again about the service, the vows, and what we think is involved—commitment, responsibilities and the like. A week before Palm Sunday Leah is higher than a kite. Her parents have said that they will come to church for the baptism even though her father hasn't been in a church "since somebody-or-other was the Pope."

On Good Friday, a gazillion people are in the service. Leah is part of the leadership. She shows up, eyes glazed over, running a whopping fever. But she does her part and heads to the doctor.

Her elder phones her parents later. They report that Leah has some bronchial infection. She needs rest and antibiotics. Leah tells the doctor, "I'll rest just as long as I can go to church on Sunday."

Sunday morning the place is a zoo. Elders giving the children who'll assist with communion last minute instructions. Visitors, kids wearing chocolate, parents of the children being baptized, grandparents glowing. Leah comes in with her parents.

Beaming is too small a word. She has on a new pair of white shoes, a gold cross her Dad has given her, and a very freshly pressed dress. During the service she is the last of six to be baptized. When I put my hand on her head I thought steam would rise. She was as hot as a firecracker but beaming from ear to ear.

I've done baptisms before when the kids were screaming their lungs out. But listening to Leah answer "I do," or "I will, God being my helper," in response to the baptismal questions, was the closest I've come to not being able to continue.

After the baptism and anointing, when the elder presented her with the certificate, candle and Bible, she could hardly believe it was for her. She looked like she had been given the greatest possible gift. And she knew it.

Who's teaching who about church here anyway? Most people think she's a nice kid. Personally I think she's a spy from God and I intend to treat her that way!

For group discussion:
What would a Sabbath year do for our congregation? What are the absolute essentials in our church?

Should we take a whole year to decide where we are going and concentrate only on that? Who would lead us through this process?

Do we need outside help? Should we ask Presbytery or one of the organizations listed on pages 133–137 to come in and help us?

Should we make a list of ten things—concrete, doable things— that we can undertake right now to prepare for the future? Or do we need more study and analysis?

Who are the people in our church who are willing to lead us into the future?

A postscript

As I think about that weekend at Cedar Glen, I wish all of us could share those kinds of experiences—where we work hard and energetically to share and gain insights about a church we love.

Such experiences can never be repeated or duplicated. But I've learned some things I can take back to my home congregation in Naramata, B.C., and I hope you've discovered some things, as you've read this book, that will be useful to you in your setting.

I hope the folks in my home congregation are willing to discuss the future and do some creative dreaming about how to get there. For such a process to succeed, it needs one or two people who will take the initiative and proceed with energy, gentleness and commitment. At the same time, it needs people with a sense of humor who won't take themselves too seriously.

Unless one or two or more people have a sense of urgency about looking at the future, or a sense of excitement, or a combination of both, it's unlikely the process will succeed. Not everyone will feel that sense of urgency, or will have the energy or interest to talk about the future. But I could invite a few people to my home one evening, read them a few selected passages from this book, share my concerns and my hopes, and then see what kind of a response I get. Then we can talk about whether we'd like to try some of the suggestions in this book, or whether we might modify them or devise our own.

Gentleness and patience are so important. There are people in our congregation who have worked hard in this church

The group that met at Cedar Glen. Front: Phyllis Airhart, Faye Wakeling, Ed Searcy; middle: Mardi Tindal, Marion Pardy, Marion Best, Allan Barss; back: Pamela Brown, Roland Kawano, Jim Sinclair.

for years. They have wisdom to offer and stories to tell. It is important to allow lots of time for each of them to tell their stories and express all their concerns.

Whether your church is in crisis and may have to close down, or whether you see the possibility of an exciting ministry ahead, in either case, something will be lost and something will be gained, and there will be grief involved. People need time and patient listeners to work through their grief.

They need an affirmation that what they worked for in the past had value. Jim Sinclair talks about a celebration of the past. When people feel valued for their contributions of the past, when they feel their fears and concerns are being taken seriously, they become much more willing to look at creative possibilities for the future. But it takes gentleness, respect, and time.

It helps to be able to "hang loose" and not take things too seriously. Creative possibilities are much more likely to emerge in an atmosphere of good humor, acceptance, and willingness to risk. Try for a framework in which people can try out ideas and let their creative juices flow. There may be times when you will need to remind folks about the topic at hand, or how much time is left, but it's best done in a good-natured way that doesn't leave anyone feeling they've been scolded.

In one sense, I feel badly that we seemed to skip over so many topics in our discussion at Cedar Glen. We all left that event with a sense that somehow we should have tied things together a bit more neatly. But we all knew that this was just the beginning of something that needed to continue in our back home settings.

We were trying to do two things at the Cedar Glen event. We were trying to offer a model of how such an event might go in your home congregation or mine. And we were hoping our discussion might stimulate your discussions.

Most of us at the Cedar Glen event seemed to feel that there is a shift going on in our church that's putting more emphasis on the congregation, and less on national and regional structures. Some of that trend is the result of tighter national and regional budgets,

The group gave Marion Best this T-shirt, in thanks for her leadership.

but some of it is because of an attitude change. If that's true, then at the local level we have to know what resources are available to strengthen and support us in our ministry and mission.

The strength of Presbyteries varies from place to place, but in every Presbytery there are capable order of ministry and lay people who are willing to share their skills and experience. Given the size of the United Church of Canada, we are wealthy in the resources available to us. There are Conference staff, in some cases Presbytery staff, Lay Centre staff, theological school faculty members, audio visual libraries, United Church book rooms, and Presbytery Resource Centres we can call upon. There's a list of some of these, starting on page 132.

So ask. A few phone calls will quickly tell you what resources you have at your disposal and what it might cost to use them.

Finally I'd like to call your attention again to the prophecy of Isaiah 43 that I quoted at the beginning of the book. There are many such hopeful and life-giving passages in the Bible and we need to call on them for strength.

> I have called you by name.
> You are mine.
> When you pass through the waters,
> I will be with you;
> and through the rivers,
> they shall not overwhelm you;
> and when you walk through fire
> you shall not be burned,
> and the flame shall not consume you.
> For I am the Lord your God,
> the Holy One of Israel,
> your Savior.

—Marion Best

Dreaming our future

An outline of six study sessions
to help your congregation make creative decisions toward a faithful future.

How to use this resource in your congregation
Every congregation in the United Church of Canada is unique.

That sounds fairly obvious, but it does mean that no "one-size-fits-all" resource will do. We can make some suggestions, but you will need to decide how best to use the resources in this book in the very unique community in which you worship.

You may wish to invite three or four active people in your congregation to read this book. Then get together over lunch or dinner, or in some other relaxed environment, and talk about next steps.

If your congregation is facing the problems that are common to most mainline churches—if you identify with many of the comments in these pages—and if people in your congregation are getting along reasonably well (no community is without a few strains and stresses), then this book could be very useful to you.

However, if you sense that the problems faced by your congregation are very complex, and if there are badly strained relationships among people, then you might suggest to your Board or Session that you ask Presbytery to provide a person to come and work with you. Or contact one of the organizations listed on pages 134–137. Most congregations can find the help if they ask for it.

In other words, there are many health-promoting things we can do by ourselves. We can treat small wounds, we can work on our diet, we can change our life-style. But if we're severely ill, we need a doctor. This book is a do-it-yourself resource for your congregation if you don't yet need the "doctor" but do sense that unless you do something creative about your future, your future will evaporate.

Some general suggestions

1. Have fun | **Have fun!** Don't take yourselves or your process too seriously so that you miss the fun and delight of being together. If, at the end of these sessions, you've simply learned to enjoy each other as people, you have a major accomplishment that will make it

Having fun is an important part of any social process. Phyllis Airhart, Ed Searcy, and Marion Best enjoy a laugh together.

possible for you to move together into your future. Do all those things that lubricate our social relationships. Meet in homes, have meals together, serve coffee, tea, juice or wine (if appropriate), tell jokes, sing songs, go for walks, be child-like.

This is worship Worship and fun are not opposites. Be sure there are opportunities for both. Begin and end with prayer, and if it feels comfortable, encourage the small groups to pray together also. Sing hymns and songs that you enjoy singing, honoring the varying tastes of your congregation.

2. Worship

The key is storytelling A congregation of the United Church is far more than an organization or a building or simply a group of people. We are a community with a history that sometimes goes back generations. All of us have feelings about why we are part of this congregation and what it means to us.

    It is essential, if we want to move into the future together, that we honor the past—honor the memories, the dedication, the people who make up the past. So however you organize your sessions, be sure to allow plenty of time for all the stories to be told, and to ensure that the rest of the community listens with interest and respect.

3. Tell stories

Don't rush decisions It's very easy to get into an argument over a specific proposal very early in the process. If that happens, you'll not really discuss the issues that move your congregation, and your "solution" will turn out to be unworkable because it was forced through too early.

    The last session in this series suggests that specific ideas might be discussed, but these will be ideas about **how** the decisions can be made, rather than the discussion of specific ideas. There will most certainly be people in the group who propose "solutions" throughout the time you spend together. When that

4. Don't rush

happens, hear the proposal in your group, write it on a flip-chart if possible, then say, "That's an interesting idea. Let's keep it so we can consider it carefully when we get to the decision-making part of our process."

5. Invite everyone

Invite everyone It is important that everyone in your congregation receives an invitation to these gatherings. We recommend the usual announcements in the bulletins and newsletters, but more importantly, each person in your congregation should receive a letter from the chair of your Board and/or a phone call inviting them to these meetings.

6. Small groups

Work in small groups Whenever possible, divide into groups of four to six people. This gives everyone a chance to talk.

7. Provide enough books

Be sure each person has a copy of this book It's important that each person read the relevant chapter before each gathering. Photocopying is illegal. Loaning books back and forth simply adds an unnecessary level of stress and complexity. Additional copies may be obtained through your United Church Publishing House outlets, through your Resource Centres, or directly from Wood Lake Books.

The sessions

We've provided general suggestions for each of the sessions on the assumption that you have some previous experience of leading a group and will add your own details. Remember, in general, that successful adult study sessions almost always involve four steps or stages: a time of gathering and getting comfortable with each other; a time for input and brainstorming; a time for intensive discussion in small groups; and a time of gathering together the learnings and discoveries.

You may consider team leadership. We're assuming you will tailor these sessions to suit your own congregation.

Session one: Gathering for the future
This would be a good time to have a pot-luck supper or a gathering will lots of social elements. If people have not had copies of this book before this meeting, hand them out now and ask them to

read chapters one and two before the next gathering.

This is a "getting-to-know-each-other" session, even if you already know each other fairly well. Ask people to talk about themselves in their small groups. Ask them to talk about those things that are most important to them. Then ask another member of that small group to introduce them to the larger group. If you have time, invite people to discuss some of the questions at the end of the chapter one.

Session two: Telling our stories

This is a continuation of session one. But this time, ask people to talk very specifically about their church background in the United Church or any other denomination. Invite them to discuss some of the questions at the end of the chapter two.

Session three: Who are we?

Using the "Reflections" in the right hand margin of the book, invite people in small groups to list ten of the most important characteristics (both good and bad) of your congregation. Ask each group to write these on sheets of newsprint. As each group reports on their discussions, post the newsprint on the wall. Then see what common themes run through all. Who are we as a church? (If possible, leave the newsprint on the wall till the next meeting. If you are meeting in the church hall, leave the sheets up so people can discuss them informally during the time between meetings.)

Session four: Potholes and pathways

Using the "Reflections" in the margins of the book, invite people in small groups to list five things that are "potholes" to a creative future for your congregation, and five things that are "pathways." Some of this will be evident from the discussion in the previous session. Again, have each group list these on newsprint, share with the larger group, post the newsprint sheets around the room, and as a large group look for common themes.

Session five: Searching the Scriptures

Each of the ten people at Cedar Glen selected a scripture passage to reflect upon. You can't all consider all of them—you won't have time—so make some choices. You could have all your groups consider one of the Cedar Glen reflections, or assign a different passage to each group. Make choices according to the needs of your congregation.

To stimulate discussion, use the reflective comments and questions in the margins of the book as well as the discussion questions at the end of the chapter. Where is God leading our congregation? Bibles (hopefully in modern translations) will be needed.

Session six: Into the future

The first question is, "How do we go about deciding what kind of a future God is calling us toward?" The second question is, "What have we learned from these discussions that should be part of our planning for the future?" Use the reflective comments in the margins of the book. Discuss these issues first in small groups, then in the larger group. Decide on your next steps.

You may wish to conclude this discussion with a celebration, perhaps a communion service.

Resources

Resources for congregations
There are many books, study guides, audio-visual tapes, periodicals, study centers and resource people available to help as you and your congregation plan for the future.

Here are some of the resources I have used in work with congregations.

Canadian Authors

Of Bodies, Priests and Stewards
by Brian Fraser   Participants book $5.00
by W. J. (Bud) Phillips   Study Guide $4.00

Available through:
> The Centre for Study of Church and Ministry
> Vancouver School of Theology
> 6000 Iona Drive
> Vancouver, B.C. V6T 1L4

This study program utilizes different biblical metaphors to engage people in an exploration of church, gospel, ministry and mission. The study guide contains step-by-step helps for leading a small group through the process in six two-hour sessions, or it can be adapted for use in a weekend retreat. This material has been used in nearly 100 congregations and the small groups have been led primarily by lay people.

The Future Church
by Douglas Hall, United Church Publishing House, $13.95

Although this book was published in 1989, it is particularly valuable for us because it is written in the Canadian context. It contains realism and hope about the future of the church as we are challenged with the responsibilities of discernment and imagination.

The important question is posed of what we need to take into the future from the past.

This United Church of Ours
by Ralph Milton, Wood Lake Books, $12.95

This is a revised edition (1991) of the best seller that was introduced in 1981. It is clear, easy reading with chapters that focus on what we believe, how we decide, and what's unique about this denomination. A study guide is available.

Where's a Good Church?
by Donald C. Posterski and Irwin Barker,
Wood Lake Books, $17.95

This book is based on a national survey of mainline and conservative church attenders. The authors asked clergy, academics, and lay members who are involved in the church what qualities matter to them. What are they looking for in their churches? What keeps them in those churches, and what drives them away?

100 Ways to Be the Church
by Clair Woodbury, Wood Lake Books, $13.95

As was evident throughout our discussions, the problems in many congregations stem from the simple diversity of their members. Communications fail and decision-making becomes a trying task. Woodbury's model helps congregations understand the dynamics of church life by focusing on lifestyle and decision-making patterns as well as identified faith stances.

Christian Parenting
by Donna Sinclair and Yvonne Stewart, Wood Lake Books, $12.95

With young families looking to the church to provide support and encouragement in child rearing, this is an important book for your congregation to make available. It addresses parenting from the perspective of Christian values in what often seems like a self-centered society. It could be used in a discussion group.

Exchange Magazine

This periodical, which is published three times a year by the national Division of Mission in Canada, is sent without charge to every United Church pastoral charge. It is filled with articles, ideas, resources for use by adults in the congregation. Ministers, Christian Education chairpersons, UCW and UCM contacts should be receiving a copy. To get on the mailing list write to:

Exchange
85 St. Clair Ave. E.
Toronto, ON M4T 1M8

Living God's Way
by Ralph Milton, Wood Lake Books, $16.95

This book contains Bible stories retold for children in today's world. It contains wonderful illustrations by Margaret Vouladakis. No matter what your age, new insights and appreciation for the biblical story and stories will emerge.

Miriam, Mary, and Me
Women in the Bible: Stories retold for children and adults
by Lois Miriam Wilson, Wood Lake Books, $19.95

This is a wonderful book for all ages but especially for parents, grandparents, teachers and the children they love and work with. Stories of women of the Bible are retold in fresh illuminating ways. Each story is accompanied by a preface for adults.

Telling Her Story:
Theology out of Women's Struggles
by Lois Miriam Wilson, United Church Publishing House, $7.95

This is an easy-to-read little book that would make an excellent study resource for those who are interested in exploring the lives of many of the little-known women of the Bible. Lois wrote this book out of her concern, as a grandmother, for passing on the Christian faith to her children and grandchildren.

Publications from the USA

Congregations: The Alban Institute

A $30.00 (US) annual membership entitles you to receive this bi-monthly journal and quarterly *Inside Information* newsletter which are filled with articles and research finding s related to mainline denominations. As a member, you also qualify for reduced rates on all Alban Institute publications and will receive an extensive catalog of resources and news of their training programs. The Institute's new address is:

    The Alban Institute
    Suite 433 North
    4550 Montgomery Ave
    Bethesda, MD 20814-3341
    Phone (301) 718-4407

The following **Alban Institute** publications are also available through United Church Bookroom outlets and Presbytery Resource Centres.

The Once and Future Church
Re-inventing the Congregation for a New Mission Frontier
by Loren Mead, Alban, $13.95 Cdn.

An easy-to-read little book that helps us to understand the depth of the changes we are experiencing. He proposes that the church as we have known it must change radically and he offers some ideas for this period between the old and the new. The main value of the book is as a discussion starter and mind expander which can prevent us from thinking that a little adjustment here and there will address the major shifts that are taking place.

A companion book by Loren Mead entitled *Transforming Congregations for the Future* will soon be available.

The Inviting Church
A Study of New Member Assimilation
by Roy Oswald and Speed Leas, Alban, $16.76 Cdn.

Does your church suffer from the revolving door syndrome? New people appear in our pews from time to time but we often don't have an effective way of incorporating them into the life of the congregation. Based on research, this book offers both an analysis of new member assimilation and some helpful suggestions.

Making Your Church More Inviting
A Step-by-Step for In-Church Training
by Roy Oswald, Alban, $20.95 Cdn.

This is a training manual that will help you put into practice the ways to invite, welcome and incorporate new members into your church.

A Lay Person's Guide to Conflict Management
by Speed Leas, Alban, $9.95 Cdn.

In times of change and stress, conflict often emerges and most congregations have difficulty both acknowledging and dealing with conflict. This little book is filled with practical, usable information that can help a congregation prevent, understand, and creatively work with conflict.

Power Analysis of a Congregation
by Roy Oswald, Alban, $8.75 Cdn.

How and by whom power and influence are exercised in the congregation greatly affects congregational life. It is also something
rarely talked about. This little workbook offers a helpful view of
power and provides a way of analyzing the power dynamics in
the congregation.

Clergy Self-Care:
Finding a Balance for Effective Ministry
by Roy Oswald, Alban, $24.95 Cdn.

This would make a wonderful gift for anyone in paid accountable
ministry. It contains self-assessment instruments and self-care
strategies to help keep one's spiritual, emotional, physical and intellectual life in balance.

Reshaping a Congregation for a New Future
by Arlin Rothauge, $8.00 Cdn.

This 30-page booklet is filled with insights, theories and suggestions for dealing with transition, whether that transition relates to
congregational size, stage of life, or changes in the surrounding
community. Available from:
> Episcopal Church Center
> 815 Second Ave.
> New York, NY 10017

Frameworks:
Patterns for Living and Believing Today
by Douglas Walrath, Pilgrim Press, $13.95 Cdn.

This book can help a congregation build understanding between
different age groups in the congregation. Walrath's theory is that
there are three different "cohort groups" which exist in both church
and society. He says a cohort is composed of contemporaries

who share experiences that uniquely and fundamentally shape them, such as the great depression of the '30s, and World War II, the affluence of the '50s and '60s, and the realization of diminishing resources in the '70s and '80s. He says because of such different formative life experiences, each of these groups has a different approach and commitment to the church and the Christian faith. Those differences often result in misunderstanding and conflict in the congregation.

How to Mobilize Church Volunteers
by Marlene Wilson, Augsburg, $13.95 Cdn.

Marlene Wilson has written numerous books on volunteers in church and community and this is one every congregation should have. Volunteers are essential to carrying out God's mission and yet most congregations could improve the way they engage, motivate, train, support, and affirm volunteers. This book is filled with practical suggestions.

Managing Transitions:
Making the Most of Change
by William Bridges, Addison Wesley, $18.95 Cdn.

While this book has been written for a secular audience, it has a useful analysis of the dynamics of change and makes the case that, while change is a rational process, transition is a psychological process that we often ignore to our peril. He gives practical advice suggestions for ways to work effectively in the midst of the three phases of transition which he describes as "endings, neutral zone, and beginnings." In the church, many of us know that something has ended but we don't have a clear picture of what the new beginning will be: thus we find ourselves in the "neutral zone" which can be both a stressful and a potentially creative place to be.

United Church Outlets

Listed below are the addresses and phone numbers of United Church outlets where all the books listed above can be obtained. In addition, in many areas of the country, there are Presbytery Resource Centres where you can purchase books.

Moncton
12 5th St.
Moncton, NB
E1E 3G9
(506) 857-9012
1-800-561-7992
fax (506) 857-9311

Montreal
301 Lansdowne Ave.
Westmount, PQ
H3Z 2L5
(514) 933-4841

Toronto
85 St. Clair Ave. E.
Toronto, ON
M4T 1M8
(416) 925-6597/925-5931
1-800-268-3781
fax (416) 925-9156

Winnipeg
120 Maryland St.
Winnipeg, MB
R3G 1L1
(204) 783-7927/786-8911
1-800-665-3391
fax (204) 775-2664

Edmonton
9919 48th Ave.
Edmonton, AB
T6E 5V6
(403) 436-4956
1-800-661-7354
fax (403) 434-4625

Vancouver
1955 West 4th Ave.
Vancouver, BC
V6J 1M7
(604) 734-0441
1-800-661-2722
fax (604) 734-0421

AVEL Resources

The following is a list of the addresses and phone numbers of the Audio Visual Education Library nearest you. They have a multitude of video cassettes that can be used for individual or group learning. Library staff can offer you help in choosing resources that will suit your needs.

St. John's AVEL Outlet
320 Elizabeth Ave.
St. John's, NF
A1B 1T9
(709) 754-0386

Maritime AVEL Outlet
564 Paul St.
Dieppe, NB
E1A 5Z1
(506) 857-9012
1-800-561-7992

Montreal AVEL Outlet
301 Lansdowne Ave.
Montreal, PQ
H3Z 2L5
(514) 933-4841

Ontario AVEL Outlet
21 Richmond St.
Brantford, ON
N3T 3X9
(519) 751-2835

Winnipeg AVEL Outlet
120 Maryland St.
Winnipeg, MB
R3G 1L1
(204) 786-8911

Edmonton AVEL Outlet
9919 48th Ave.
Edmonton, AB
T6E 5V6
(403) 434-2036

Vancouver AVEL Outlet
103-1955 West 4th Ave.
Vancouver, BC
V6J 1M7
(604) 734-7133

Continuing Education Opportunities and Resource People

Our church has a wide range of people and places available to us to assist with learning. If it's too hard for you to travel there, ask them to come to you.

Did you know there is continuing education funding assistance available for lay people as well as for order of ministry people? The Life Long Learning Fund will assist you to take courses or help you bring resource people to your community. Your minister will have the address and phone number of your Conference Office where you can inquire further.

Each of the 13 Conferences in the United Church have staff people with expertise and resources to help your congregation.

Find out what they have to offer.

Listed below are the addresses and phone numbers of United Church learning centers. The lay training centers and the theological schools offer programs for both ordered and lay people. Write to them and ask for an outline of the current season's programs. Many of them make their staff available for workshops and seminars in local communities.

Theological Colleges

Atlantic School of Theology, Pine Hill Divinity Hall
640 Francklyn St.
Halifax, NS
B3H 3B5
(902) 423-6939
fax (902) 492-4048

Centre for Christian Studies
77 Charles St. W.
Toronto, ON
M5S 1K5
(416) 923-1168
fax (416) 923-5496

Emmanuel College
75 Queen's Park Crescent
Toronto, ON
M5S 1K7
(416) 585-4539
fax (416) 585-4584

Queen's Theological College
Queen's University
Kingston, ON
K7L 3N6
(613) 545-2110
fax (613) 545-6300

St. Andrew's College
1121 College Dr.
Saskatoon, SK
S7N 0W3
(306) 966-8970
fax (306) 966-6575

St. Stephen's College
University of Alberta
8810-112th St.
Building 59
Edmonton, AB
T6G 2J6
(403) 439-7311
fax (403) 433-8875

United Theological College
3521 rue University
Montreal, PQ
H3A 2A9
(514) 849-2042
fax (514) 398-6665

University of Winnipeg
Faculty of Theology
515 Portage Ave.
Winnipeg, MB
R3B 2E9
(204) 786-7811
fax (204) 783-4781

Vancouver School of Theology
6000 Iona Dr.
Vancouver, BC
V6T 1L4
(604) 228-9031
fax (604) 228-0189

Continuing Education and Lay Training Centres

Five Oaks Christian Workers Centre
Box 216
Paris, ON
N3L 3E7
(519) 442-3212
fax (510) 442-3444

Naramata Centre
Box 68
Naramata, BC
V0H 1N0
(604) 496-5751
fax (604) 496-5800

Prairie Christian Training Centre (PCTC)
Box 159
Fort Qu'Appelle, SK
S0G 1S0
(306) 332-5691
fax (306) 332-5532

Stuart House
Box 119
Pakenham, ON
K0A 2X0
(613) 624-5317
fax (613) 254-2073

Tatamagouche Centre
Altantic Christian Training Centre (ACTC)
R. R. 3
Tatamagouche, NS
B0K 1V0
(902) 657-2231
fax (902) 657-3600

Study Resource Centres

Francis Sandy Native Training Centre
Box 446
Paris, ON
N3L 3T5
(519) 442-7725,
fax (519) 442-3444

Iona College
University of Windsor
Windsor, ON
N9B 3A7
(519) 973-7039
fax (519) 973-7050

Dr. Jessie Saulteaux Resource Centre
Box 210
Beausejour, MB
R0E 0C0
(204) 268-3913
fax (204) 268-4463

The Centre for Study of Church and Ministry
Vancouver School of Theology
6000 Iona Dr.
Vancouver, BC
V6T 1L4
(604) 228-9031
fax (604) 228-0189

The TEE Centre (Theological Education by Extension)
4506 Lakelse Ave., S-C,
Terrace, BC
V8G 1P4
(604) 635-6285
fax (604) 635-9582